MW00573161

THE
SHAMAN'S
BOOK OF
EXTRAORDINARY
PRACTICES

THE
SHAMAN'S
BOOK OF
EXTRAORDINARY
PRACTICES

58 Power Tools for
PERSONAL TRANSFORMATION

JOSÉ LUIS STEVENS, PhD

Hierophantpublishing

Copyright © 2024 by José Luis Stevens

The practices presented in this book are not intended to substitute
for professional counseling or medical treatment. Consult a
healthcare professional for personalized guidance.

All rights reserved, including the right to reproduce this work
in any form whatsoever, without permission in writing from the
publisher, except for brief passages in connection with a review.

Cover design by Adrian Morgan
Cover art by CreativeNature_nl and Shutterstock
Print book interior design by Frame25 Productions

Hierophant Publishing
San Antonio, TX
www.hierophantpublishing.com

If you are unable to order this book from your local bookseller,
you may order directly from the publisher.

Library of Congress Control Number: 2024935586
ISBN: 978-1-950253-53-1

10 9 8 7 6 5 4 3 2 1

Contents

Part Six: Perceptual Practices

Introduction

Have you ever found yourself wanting to practice something in order to enjoy it more, increase your skills, or ultimately master it? Believe it or not, most people like to practice and do it every day in one way or another, because it is so central to being human.

We practice telling jokes or what we will say in an interview. We practice speaking foreign languages, playing the guitar, carving wood, or tying knots. We work at playing chess, or driving golf balls, or making free throws. We practice yoga asanas, or a million other things, like trying on expressions in the mirror when we are kids, or trying on different outfits to look and feel better. We all have our favorite things to practice and this is how we improve and widen our worlds. It is how we ultimately get enormous satisfaction from our activities.

This is a book about shamanic and mystical practices, loaded with information to help you rapidly change your life for the better, perhaps even radically.

You can do these practices often, occasionally, or, in some cases, only once.

I know all these practices work remarkably well because I have tested each and every one of them, most over many years. While there are other powerful shamanic practices, I have selected those that can be done rather quickly and, in my view, easily. Nonetheless, I want to be clear that these practices all require your involvement. Just reading about them is not enough, although it is a good start.

I introduce each practice with commentary that is designed to set the stage for performing it. And, in some cases, the practice itself is much shorter than the commentary. I include this information because I have found it can be quite helpful in establishing the purpose and context of the practice, thereby making it more valuable for you.

Most of these practices originate in ancient wisdom traditions like shamanism. Some come from oral traditions. Others come from Buddhism, Taoism, Islam, and Christianity. Some are practices I developed myself, with the goal of addressing a particular need I perceived within myself or among my many shamanic students. Regardless of their source, however, they can all wake you up and give you a much-needed boost—physically, mentally, emotionally, and spiritually.

These practices have improved my physical health, filled me with joy, and enriched my relationships. Moreover, I've seen the tremendous benefits they've brought to my students—accelerating spiritual growth, dissolving fear, and opening hearts to the unconditional love that is our birthright. I hope you have fun with them and gain great value by exploring them.

Over the course of my life, I have read many books that included spiritual practices, many of which are quite complicated. You won't find any of these in this book, however. The practices given here are relatively simple to perform but can produce revolutionary results. That means you will have to be prepared to adapt to the changes they bring about. Almost all of them require no more than ten or fifteen minutes of your time, some much less. The few that are longer I include because I feel they are foundational.

If you were to do many of these practices every day, it would take up to several hours. Since this may be unrealistic for some of you, you can just concentrate on one or two at a time and still gain great benefit. Most of them are actually quite enjoyable to do. I myself devote many hours each day to performing them because I find them such compelling, wonderful teachers. I don't grit my teeth to do them. In fact, some have become second nature to me and are just part of the fabric of my daily life. I feel truly blessed to have come across them. I hope you will feel the same.

Some of you may already know where my focus lies. For those of you who are new to my work, let me share a little about my philosophy and orientation. I am a student of shamanism, mysticism, and alchemical processes from various traditions—among them Buddhism, Hinduism, Christian mysticsm, Taoism, and Sufism. I like to study the lives of shamans, mystics, saints, and avatars, and am very interested in the teachings of adepts who "know." I have always been a respectful student and explorer of altered states of awareness.

Although I was once an anxious child and a depressed teenager, these studies have helped me transform into the highly inspired and optimistic elder I am today—a sought-after spiritual guide, counselor, and teacher. As cofounders of the Power Path School of Shamanism, my wife and I have helped thousands of people access their higher wisdom, discover their life purpose, and awaken to their divine nature through books, articles, webinars, and retreats. Here are three important lessons I have learned as I've traveled this path:

- Contrary to what many believe, it's the little things that make all the difference in life.

- Contrary to what many believe, it need not cost a fortune or require a huge effort to transform your life. It just takes interest, focus, and some dedication.

- ◆ Contrary to what many believe, you can transform your life by investing only a few minutes several times a day.

To benefit from this book, all you need is an open mind, a sense of curiosity, and a willingness to experiment. You are already perfect, but sometimes we all need help remembering that. I hope that this book will help you rediscover your perfect self. And if it proves valuable to you, it may also prove valuable to others. So please share what you learn here, and perhaps even give this book as a gift to those you know.

About This Book

Think of this book as a treasure chest that you can delve into at your leisure. You don't need to read the practices in any specific order, and there is no progression from least to most important. Some you will find simpler and some more challenging. For the sake of convenience, I've organized the practices into six categories:

- ◆ Preparatory practices that help you establish a set of basic spiritual skills.

- ◆ Energetic practices that help you unblock and redirect stuck energy.

- Relational practices that invoke and make sacred your relationships with others, with Spirit, with plants and animals, and with yourself.

- Physical practices that use your body as a portal to the divine.

- Creative practices that use the power of your imagination to promote spiritual growth.

- Perceptual practices that teach you new ways of seeing the world around you.

Start with what calls to you the most strongly, then jump forward or backward from there.

You will soon discover that these categories are very loose. After all, every one of these practices has a physical component (because we are always in our bodies), a perceptual component (because we are always perceiving), and a relational component (because we are always in a state of relationship). Every one of them can be considered preparatory, in the sense that they prepare you to take a deeper dive into whatever spiritual vein feels richest to you. They are all creative, in the sense that we never leave home without our imaginations. They are all energetic, in the sense that life is no more and no less than a constant state of moving energy around.

My hope is that these practices will unlock your potential for growth. As more and more human beings wake up, our shared future becomes brighter and brighter. It makes me happy to think that this book may play some small role in that process of evolution.

PART ONE

Preparatory Practices

Although all the practices in this book can be considered prepa-
ratory, in the sense that any one of them can act as a wonder-
ful starting point for personal transformation, the practices in
Part One have a special ability to wake you up and sharpen your
awareness. By working with them, you train yourself to see the
world through shamanic eyes—as a vast, interconnected web of
being that responds to you, just as you are constantly responding
to it. These practices teach you that your inner world is a mirror
of the external world, and vice versa. This simple realization is
the foundation of all spiritual growth.

The Extraordinary Practice of Saying Hello

Many years ago, I was traveling in Nepal as one of the principal guides for a group of twenty people. We were in the Everest Base Camp region, headed for a particular village where we were to meet a local shaman for a ceremony. On our way, we passed a large monastery where we stopped briefly to rest. The lama who greeted us said that all the people there were participating in a silent retreat, but were nevertheless interested in meeting us because they received so few visitors from the outside world. It would be a special treat, he said, for them to greet us silently.

When we readily agreed, the lama had us stand outside the front door of the monastery. Lamas, monks, and ordinary-looking Nepalese people came filing out and stood as a group to greet us. Out of respect for their vow of silence, they spoke no words, and we refrained from speaking as well. But their faces were joyous; ear-to-ear smiles expressed their total gladness at meeting us. Soon, we were grinning in a similar way and making eye contact with them in one of the most intimate greetings I have ever experienced.

We stood there for about twenty minutes in total silence, just being with one another in a spontaneous love fest. We couldn't speak to one another, but we were saying "hello" with our hearts and spirits. No one wanted to leave, but at a certain point the lama who had first greeted us announced that it was time for the retreat particpants to go back inside, and so we resumed our walk to our destination for the day. This amazing experience left me in a completely altered state, and I have never forgotten those beautiful people whom we did not even know. Even today, the memory of it brings tears to my eyes.

In Nepal and throughout the Himalayas, people greet each other by folding their hands, bowing slightly, and saying *Namaste*. Roughly translated, this greeting means: "The Spirit that is within me acknowledges the same Spirit that is within you." Similarly, in Central America, people of Mayan origins greet each other with the phrase *In Lak'ech Ala K'in*, which roughly means: "I am you and you are me." For them, saying "hello" is more than a simple spoken greeting. It is an acknowledgment of something much more profound, something grounded in a central truth.

No matter where you travel in the world, when you meet people, the first thing you do is say "hello." If you don't know how to say it in their language, you smile at them, indicating that you are friendly and want to make a positive connection. We say "hello" because we want to open a conversation, or ask a question, or engage in a transaction, or just acknowledge another's presence in a kind and respectful way. In day-to-day life, saying "hello" can be a simple social courtesy. But at its deepest level, saying "hello" can be a sacred act of witnessing.

When someone greets you with warmth and kindness, you perk up and feel more awake, more grounded, and more attuned. Believe it or not, this phenomenon is not limited to human beings. Everything in nature responds to being greeted in a friendly way. You may not be able to see it with your naked eye, but when monitoring equipment is hooked up to plants, it clearly shows that they respond to greetings. Animals also recognize when you greet them. So do trees, the breeze, streams, and everything else in your environment. Whatever you greet becomes more friendly to you and greets you back in some favorable way. You could even say that your greetings are taken as blessings and that you are blessed back many times over!

The practice that follows consists of simply saying "hello" to everything you encounter, whether it's a raven, an oak tree, a rock, the breeze, a cloud, your house, or the road. By greeting everything you encounter respectfully, no matter what it is, you remind yourself that you are surrounded by other forms of life and other forms of consciousness, even subatomic materials that make up man-made objects.

I have studied with the Wixarika, a Toltec tribe in Mexico, for many years. The Wixarika, referred to by Mexicans as *Huichols*, believe that you should communicate with your tools and even bless them and feed them with corn pollen or drops of blessed water so that they will perform better for you. They consider everything to be alive. That is a stretch for some of us who have been educated very differently, especially those from Western traditions. But I do offer my car tobacco and ask for protection and safe travel, and it seems to work very well. You can decide for yourself what feels appropriate for you.

Practice: Greeting the World

This practice can make a huge difference in your day. I find that it helps me pay more attention to the beauty and life all around me and changes my mood in a positive way. It also reminds me that Spirit is everywhere around me all the time and is saying "hello" back to me with blessings.

1. Every morning when you wake up, go out and spend the first few minutes of your day saying "hello" to every living thing you see or any natural aspects of nature you experience. Don't hesitate to say "hello" to man-made objects like your car, your house, and perhaps tools you use as well. They, like everything else, are made up of Spirit.

2. Say "hello" to the environment—to the sky, the clouds, the breeze, and the birds; to the trees, the bushes, the grasses, the flowers, and the minerals in the earth; to the earthworms and insects that you know are there but may not be able to see; to the dewdrops on plants or any standing water.

3. Say "hello" to the sun, to the moon, and to any stars and planets that are still visible. In fact, say it to the stars and planets even if you cannot see them, because they are very much there.

4. Say "hello" to things that are unseen but still very present—hibernating animals, roots of trees, layers of earth and rock, birds high up in the trees. Say it to the forest as it stretches beyond the horizon and to nearby communities

that you can't see. Continue these greetings for as long as you like—perhaps ten minutes.

5. Once you have finished with your greetings, tell everything how beautiful it is and how much you appreciate it being there. Acknowledge the sun for warming you and shedding its light. Thank your house for providing shelter; thank your car or bike for transporting you. Allow yourself to feel true wonder and appreciation for all these things. Smile and speak kindly to them, as if they are good friends you are happy to see. If you don't have access to the outdoors, look out a window or go out on a balcony. Be creative.

Begin by doing this practice for a few minutes each morning. Eventually, you may find yourself doing it throughout the day. When it becomes second nature to you, you move through the world as a friend to all that exists. This practice puts you back in touch with Spirit and reminds you that you are a part of the web of life, the whole universe, not apart from it.

The Extraordinary Practice
of Greeting the Body

We are blessed to live in an age when people are becoming more aware of their health. Fewer people than ever are smoking; younger generations are drinking less alcohol; more people than ever are taking up yoga, plant-based diets, and other healthy habits. All over the world, people are waking up to the fact that their bodies are more than just machines to be used and abused in the name of extracting maximum productivity. Quite the opposite is true: our bodies are exquisitely complex organisms, and have more in common with coral reefs than with mechanical devices.

A coral reef is a living system composed of a dizzying array of living elements, all working together for maximum health and life. In much the same way, our bodies are not just one solid lump—although we may be accustomed to experiencing them that way. Rather, they are a teeming diversity of organs, bacteria, microflora, viruses, and archaea. In fact, according to one source, more than half the human body is not, strictly speaking, human at all. We share about 50 percent of our DNA with trees, 60 percent with bananas, and 70 percent with slugs!

Once you begin to delve into the wonders of the human body, it's hard not to be filled with a sense of awe and gratitude for the experience of being alive. Our bodies are masterpieces of evolution, shaped over millions of years to support the miracle of human consciousness. Every cell, every organ, and every system has been finely tuned to work in harmony with all the others. When we bring curiosity and wonder to exploring our physical selves, it can open up new dimensions of health and wholeness.

In the previous practice, you learned the extraordinary power of greeting everything in your external environment. The following practice will show you how to turn this same technique inward, greeting the parts of yourself that you normally ignore. Many of us never think to be grateful for our lungs, kidneys, teeth, or pancreas, and yet they serve us every moment of every day. Many of us never think to say a friendly "thank you" to the flora in our guts or the bacteria on our skin. By turning your loving attention to all these elements of life, you can learn to treasure them more deeply.

From a shamanic perspective, your body is an ally—or, more accurately, a set of allies. In many ways, it is your most intimate and powerful ally because without it, you just cannot have the experience of being human. Shamans honor their allies, give them offerings, and thank them repeatedly. Think of this practice as a way of making these offerings and expressing your gratitude for services rendered, all with a simple greeting.

Try not to think of the parts of your body as objects or things. They are more like energetic processes that together form a symphony. They are not as physical as we tend to think. They are concentrations of awareness, consciousness, and the presence of Spirit within. In the end, this consciousness, this Spirit, outlasts the body because our awareness is independent of and exists beyond our body parts.

But that does not mean that we should not be grateful to our bodies for their service. And the truth is that, like any pet, the more attention we pay to our bodies in a good way, the happier and more responsible they will be. They are here to serve and that is what makes them happy. If our bodies are not well, that is not their fault. They are only following our instructions, and if we mistreat them, they will suffer.

Practice: Greeting Your Body

I developed this practice as a way of getting to know my body in intimate detail, and it has brought me peace, good health, and an enduring sense of gratitude and awe.

1. Find a comfortable place to sit or lie down.

2. Starting with your head, move slowly down through your body, sincerely acknowledging every body part you can identify. You can name whole systems, skipping the individual parts, or you can name each part individually, depending on your knowledge of anatomy or your time. For example:

- Hello mouth, teeth, gums, tongue, lips.

- Hello jaw, inner ears, ears, nose, and sinuses.

- Hello eyes, brain, brain stem, central nervous system, endocrine system, immune system, reproductive and digestive systems, cardiovascular and respiratory systems, limbic system, muscular and skeletal systems.

- Hello pineal and pituitary glands, and corpus collosum.

- Hello right and left hemispheres of the brain.

- Hello hippocampus and amygdala, learning and memory functions.

- Hello cerebellum and fine motor movements of the body.

- Hello thalamus, hypothalamus, and medulla.

- Hello frontal, occipital, temporal, parietal, and limbic lobes.

- Hello all white matter and gray matter.

- Hello thyroid, thymus, adrenals, and kidneys.

- Hello pancreas, gallbladder, liver, and spleen.

- Hello vocal cords, bronchial tubes, lungs, esophagus, stomach.

- Hello upper and lower intestines, bladder, rectum, genitals, womb and ovaries, perineum.

- Hello cervical, thoracic, and lumbar vertebrae, coccyx and whole back.

- Hello interconnective tissue, skin, hair, nails.

- Hello toes, feet, ankles, and shins, calves, knees, and hamstrings.

- Hello pelvis, solar plexus, navel.

- Hello heart, chest, throat.

- Hello fingers, hands, wrists, and fore-arms, elbows, upper arms, and shoulders.

- Hello DNA and all the cells of my body.

- Hello atomic structure of my body.

- Hello to all the parts I have not named.

- Thank you for all working together for my great benefit.

- Many blessings to all of you. I love you.

As a variation on this practice, you can make an assertion like: "I renew, restore, refresh, and revitalize my knees." Or "I renew, restore, refresh, and revitalize my bones." As you do so, imagine these body parts being filled with health and life.

The Extraordinary Practice of Cultivating Gratitude, Love, and Awe

A great teacher once told me: "If you want to experience rapid, enduring, and powerful transformation, practice gratitude, love, and awe." These three states have been cultivated by all the great saints from a wide range of spiritual traditions over millennia. Each one of them expands your heart and stretches you without fail. In shamanic terms, they are considered to be "great medicines."

What do gratitude, love, and awe have in common? They tend to beget more of the same when we focus on them, and they are pure gold when it comes to attracting the most wonderful experiences in life. They are all high-vibration, expansive states. Just as pure water, rich soil, and sunlight cause flowers to grow, gratitude, love, and awe lead us to blossom with generosity, benevolence, and selflessness, while letting go of our self-centered view of reality. An egoic, contracted mind thinks: "I don't have enough." A grateful mind perceives the abundance of Spirit everywhere. A contracted mind thinks: "You're not good enough—and I'm not either." A loving mind sees the beauty and worth in every living being. A contracted mind is bored, impatient, and restless. A mind touched by awe is awake to the divinity in every moment.

The truth is that human beings are wired for happiness, in the same way a house is wired for light. Our brains and bodies have all the right equipment built in for feeling good—we don't need to go looking for positive feelings somewhere else. With a little bit of practice, we can all learn (or relearn) how to activate this standard-issue hardware, and enjoy the expansive states that were ours all along.

The practices below are among my favorites, because they are so very simple and yet they can completely transform your life. You don't need to be an expert meditator or an advanced yogi to benefit from them. In fact, the more childlike you can become, the better they work. There is nothing more important and powerful than gratitude, love, and awe to transform your experience, raise your awareness, and open the door to your highest state of evolution. There is no way these practices can fail, and they produce immediate results.

Gratitude

The fourth-century BCE Greek philosopher Plato is credited with saying: "A grateful mind is a great mind that eventually attracts to itself great things." Although it's unclear whether or not Plato ever wrote or said these actual words, we do know that he believed that by focusing our thoughts and attention on higher virtues, we can orient our lives toward truth and goodness. As a result of cultivating this harmonious state, we also place ourselves in the path of everything good and beautiful—attracting to ourselves great things.

Gratitude is a state of awareness in which you truly and sincerely appreciate the gifts of your life and express that appreciation on a regular basis—by saying a sincere "thank you" to the people around you, by praying and making offerings, by paying forward the gifts you have received, or by a thousand other means. Gratitude is magnetic. It demonstrates the natural law that like attracts like. Simply put, gratitude attracts more gratitude to itself. When you feel grateful, Spirit takes notice. It's as if God says: "Oh, you are feeling grateful! Here, have some more experiences like this one." Before long, you have even more to feel grateful for. And when you feel grateful for these new conditions or situations, the same process takes place all over again. You are enriched again and again, until you feel grateful a much higher percentage of the time.

There are some attitudes that can get in the way of being grateful, however, and these must be dealt with first. These include arrogance and narcissism, a sense of entitlement, and feeling that the world owes you a living. Perhaps the worst obstacle of all is an attitude of victimization and martyrdom. Feeling resentful and victimized by life cuts you off from genuine gratitude, because it is hard to let go of the juiciness of feeling sorry for yourself and blaming others for your misery.

Dealing with these obstacles can take a considerable amount of work, but they have to be dealt with in order for you to get the benefits of gratitude. Otherwise, you are just fooling yourself by mouthing platitudes. Something has to go—your happiness or your misery. In the end, you can't have both. You must choose one or the other. If you find any of these traits in yourself, start releasing them right now. Just observe the tendencies and directly address the ungrateful thoughts by saying: "You have no power over me. Leave now!" You could call that a preliminary practice.

You may be thinking that this sounds really corny and oversimplified, and that it can't be that simple. *Oh yes it can.* Sometimes we simply don't see things that are right in front of our faces because we are too close to them. This next practice can help you become more aware of how these negative attitudes are influencing your life and teach you how to overcome them, so that you can initiate and maintain the "virtuous cycle" of gratitude.

Practice: Inviting Abundance into Your Life

This practice teaches you how to invite more and more abundance into your life. The key to its success is the sincerity of your gratitude and the intensity with which you feel it.

1. Identify anything in your life for which you feel grateful, whether it was given to you by others or you acquired it through your own efforts. It doesn't matter what it is, as long as you feel happy that it is in your life and sense its value—good health, a loving spouse, good friends, a great job or income, a wonderful dog or cat, the fact that the sun is out or that you had a great night's sleep. Anything will do. Notice that when you focus on what makes you feel grateful, it creates a very specific kind of sensation in you—the vibration of gratitude. We tend to identify this as an emotion, but it is more than any ordinary feeling.

2. Compare what you are experiencing in your body and senses after you have completed your list with how you felt when you started it. You

may find that you feel an actual buzzing sensation or feel lit up like a bright light. Notice that this is expansive and not constrictive, as many thoughts and feelings are.

3. If you find yourself drifting away from gratitude after a difficult experience, ask your allies or guides to help you bring it back.

4. Realize that all of creation is supporting your life here on earth. Allow this awareness to saturate your mind in the radiance of gratitude. And remember that the more grateful you feel, the more experiences you will attract into your life for which you will, in turn, feel grateful.

With gratitude in your heart, you can do so much more in your life—take more risks, connect more with others, and attract the right people and situations to you. Think of gratitude as a powerful ally that accompanies you through your life, and remember to be grateful that gratitude has become a part of your path.

Love

When I was in my twenties, I traveled on my own throughout India and Nepal for four months. I stayed in Katmandu for almost a month and serendipitously found a Tibetan Buddhist lama with whom to study. Every day, I visited him in his monastery on top of a high hill. For a couple of hours each morning, he taught me about the basics of Tibetan Buddhism in his broken English. Then I spent the rest of each day contemplating his teachings as I wandered around Katmandu.

After a month, I felt the call to continue my travels, having never intended to linger so long in one place. As I told the lama that I was moving on and thanked him profusely, I was amazed to find that I teared up and felt an enormous love for him that came upon me quite unexpectedly. He smiled brightly and approached me, putting his forehead on mine. We stayed that way for some time. Then he blessed me and I bid him goodbye. I cried a torrent of tears afterward, not knowing how I had developed such strong feelings of love in such a short time. I felt more love for this man than for anyone I had ever known in my life.

At the time, I didn't realize that this seemingly accidental relationship was actually a form of agreement. This teacher knew I was coming. He did not try to stop me from leaving. It was only later that I realized that I knew him from a past life. The touching of our foreheads was revealed to me as a tremendous download and transmission that changed my life from that point on. Little did I know at the time what a powerhouse this lama actually was. As I write this over fifty years later, I find myself tearing up again at the profound feelings of love I still have for him.

Think about the most profound experience of love you've ever had—the first time you held your newborn baby, or when a friend held you tightly as you grieved, or when you gazed into your lover's eyes in a moment of complete vulnerability and felt as if everything was right with the world. Perhaps it was an experience you yourself had with a spiritual teacher. Love has an extraordinary ability to make small, everyday concerns fall away, restoring us to our true center. When we operate from a state of love, actions and decisions flow naturally. The path seems to unfold before our eyes, and we become completely available to all the beauty that life has to offer.

Although we may feel intense love for a specific person, the great spiritual masters have always taught that we can learn to feel this same love for all people. Indeed, by some definitions, this is what it means to be enlightened. Imagine walking through the world and feeling the same intense love for the strangers on the street that you feel for your own children. How would that change your actions and decisions throughout the day? Now imagine that you allowed yourself to feel that strangers on the street love you that much as well. How would that change you? Would your fears, anxieties, and woundedness begin to drop away?

What if you walked on a beach and felt that the sea and the sand and the whole sky love you unconditionally? What if you felt the love of the forest, the love of the trees for each other or for the sun and sky toward which they reach? What if you realized the secret that Einstein kept hidden for so long and that was only revealed in his writings after his death—that it is actually *love* that equals MC²?

Practice: Letting Love In

Love is everywhere, in everything. We just need to take down the barriers we've erected against it and let it into our lives. This practice shows you how to dissolve these barriers, opening yourself to more and more of the love that surrounds you at all times.

1. Focus on people, animals, places, events, and experiences that you know you love without question.

2. What sensation do you experience as you go over each item on your list? What sets this experience apart from any other experience? Feel the quality of it, the sensations in your body as you contemplate your loved ones and places. Where do you feel these sensations in

your body? Do words adequately convey what you feel, what you experience?

3. Notice that the feeling is expansive, even grand, maybe even a little scary, as if you don't know what to do with so much love in you. Notice that love is more than a feeling—that it is, in fact, a high vibration.

4. Notice that too much attachment to the thing you say you love tends to interfere with the wonderful sensation and turns it into something that may have fear associated with losing it.

5. See if you can be neutral about what you love, in the sense of not craving it. Just let the love be there and be present with it. Animals are useful to focus on here, because there is no possibility of developing a complicated romantic attraction. Animals are just very lovable in a simple sort of way.

6. Notice that the love you feel for these various expressions of Spirit is inside of you and not exactly with the object of your love. *You* are the love you love. And the love you love is made possible by the source of all love, Spirit itself.

7. Notice that love is not one thing, but many things. It is magnetic and draws to you those things and people for whom you feel love, making you want to embrace them. Yet sometimes love means letting go, even though you may want to hold on to the object of your love.

8. Try giving what you love the freedom to just be—as when you let your growing children or students become independent of you to learn their own lessons. Let go of any conditions you may demand or require of others to earn your love. Let your love be free and let others be as they are, not as you want them to be. Explore any tendencies you may have to make your love conditional. No blame. Just observe and notice.

9. Try saying: "I am loved by Spirit." Or "I am known by Spirit and Spirit loves me without any reservation and without limit." Then substitute the object of your love for the word "Spirit": "I am loved by [your object]." Or "[Your object] is known by me and is loved by me without any reservation or limitation."

The more you allow yourself to experience the vibration of love, the more you attract people, events, and other things that you love as well. The more things you love in your life, the richer your life will become. If you experiment with this, you will find that love grows very rapidly—like a fast-growing plant.

The deeper you go with this practice, the more evident it becomes that human consciousness is a river of love flowing through you, whether you notice it or not. You are, literally, composed of the vibration of love. It is who you are, what you are, at the subatomic level. Realizing this enlightens you and brings great joy.

Awe

Have you ever wondered why your jaw drops when you see a stunning sight or experience something incredible? That's because our jaws are linked to our sense of stability. When we feel threatened or defensive, we hold our jaws tight, because it gives us a sense of control. But when we feel amazed or overcome by wonder, we loosen our jaws involuntarily, because we are so overcome with delight that we drop our need to control. When we are awestruck, we blurt out words like "Wow!" or "Whoa!" or "Holy Moly!" That is because, for a brief moment, we have let go of controlling ourselves and allowed ourselves to be completely authentic.

Being thunderstruck from time to time—or gobsmacked, as the Irish say—is a good thing for us humans. It stretches our sense of what's possible, and helps us grow to accommodate new things. Whether we are watching incredible feats at the circus or gazing up at the northern lights on a wintry night, when we are overcome with amazement, it restores our sense of joy and wonder. Awe is an altered state, one that inspires us, pulls us out of the doldrums, and lifts us up. And remember that it always takes some kind of altered state to heal ourselves, because we must step out of the known, however briefly. Therefore, awe is healing.

I once met a man who held the Guinness world record as the strongest man in the world. He put on an amazing performance right in front of me, balancing on a knifepoint on his belly. I watched as he danced on flaming shards of glass that he shattered. I saw him lift impossibly heavy objects as if they weighed nothing, and act as a human magnet, holding metal objects all over his body and then letting them all drop to the floor. This man was not just strong—he was what many would call supernatural!

I was thrilled by this demonstration, because it made me realize that if he could do those things, any human could do them with the proper skills and training. It destroyed the narrow ideas I had of what was and wasn't possible. I had lunch with him afterward and discovered what a humble, kind, and compassionate human being he was, and I was even more delighted to learn how normal he was.

Since then, I have witnessed many other events that I thought were impossible—people walking on blazing hot coals; a mystic pushing knitting needles through his body and healing instantly from the wounds; a Chinese healer visibly shrinking a woman's tumor by simply talking to it, monitored by ultrasound; Buddhists in Thailand stabbing themselves with swords and knives during a special ceremony and healing instantly; a Filipino psychic surgeon pulling out tumors with his fingers, and on and on. And then there were amazing animal events like the spectacular red-tailed hawk that flew right in front of the bride and groom at an outdoor wedding I was officiating; or the monster elk with the huge rack that I startled in the forest who ran at me at top speed and blew by me as if I were a matador at a bullfight; or the king cobra that dropped out of the ceiling in a ruined monastery in Cambodia and landed at my feet; or the massive whale that breached next to my boat in Mexico. Gobsmacked. Awestruck. Over and over. And yet these types of experiences are possible any day of our lives.

But you don't have to watch someone dance on shards of glass or walk over hot coals, or even meet a cobra in a ruin, in order to connect with a sense of awe. All you have to do is contemplate your own aliveness to discover something absolutely amazing— your own awareness, your own presence, your own consciousness. How did you get here? How did that happen? Where did you come from? Is it an accident? Try to wrap your mind around the idea of infinity—no end, no limit, forever and ever, infinite space. Contemplate the universe. Consider universes stacked by the trillions, all with slight variations, yet no two alike. Try to comprehend trillions and trillions of parallel universes all coexisting and allowing for every possibility to play out to completion, and each one spawning trillions more, every second, eternally. How could that be? Whose idea was this anyway?

The following practice can help open your awareness to these sorts of wonders and reawaken your sense of awe—an expansive state in which all things are possible, and all preconceptions fall away.

Practice: Reawakening Your Sense of Awe

There is no better place to go to put yourself in the path of awe than nature. Your local forest, desert, or wetland is filled with awe-inspiring sights. It's only a matter of opening your eyes to see them.

1. Head to a natural area. You can bring binoculars, a magnifying glass, a sketchbook, or any other tool that might inspire you to slow down and turn your full attention to the natural world. You may also want to bring a small offering like

flowers or tobacco to signal your intention to be fully present with the wonders around you.

2. Find a place to sit, with the intention of remaining there for at least twenty minutes. Then simply look around, allowing yourself to notice things that you would normally be too busy or preoccupied to see.

3. Take a close look at the thick oyster mushroom growing out of a decaying log. Pay close attention to a birdsong so that you hear each individual note. If you are sitting near a lake or stream, watch the movement of the water, letting it dazzle you with its infinite variations. Take off your shoes and step into a river, realizing that the same person never steps into the same river twice. Such is our rate of transformation on this planet.

4. Lie on your back and watch the sky, the clouds building, the flocks of starlings that move as one. Incredible.

5. Allow yourself to sink into the sense of awe in the same way you may have when you were a child, without trying to analyze what you are

seeing or worrying about the "more important" things you ought to be doing. Remember that being alive truly is a wonder in itself, and that wonder is always available to you when you make space for it.

6. As you go about the rest of your day, see if you can access the same sense of awe you found in nature. Can you feel awe toward the bug crawling across your desk, or the potted plant blooming on your windowsill? Can you feel awe when you see a beautiful old babushka feeding the pigeons popcorn in the park? Or a bunch of first graders laughing and giggling as school lets out? Can you feel awe at the dewdrops shining like crystals on a web after a morning shower?

7. Contemplate your hands in great detail and feel all the sensations. Can you imagine being without them? Take extraordinary delight in them. Such amazing creations! Do this with your tongue, teeth, eyes, feet, toes, or whatever you are drawn to contemplate.

Use your experiences in nature as a bridge to feeling awe wherever you are.

The Extraordinary Practice
of Returning to Neutral

The beloved Zen text *Hsing Hsing Ming* contains this famous passage: "The Great Way is not difficult for those who have no preferences. . . . Make the smallest distinction, however, and heaven and earth are set infinitely apart."

In other words, if you want to align yourself with the Tao (aka with Spirit, Source, God, or whatever word you prefer to use for the divine), the first step is to let go of your addiction to your own personal dramas—the parts of you that say: "Hey, I don't like this!" Or "Wait, I really want what he's got!" Or "I'll look really important if I do this." Whenever we express a preference—the preference to be comfortable instead of uncomfortable, famous instead of obscure, or even beloved instead of simply tolerated—we say "no" to some aspect of life. Instead of embracing life in all its vastness, we try to shrink it down to a size and shape we can understand, or that flatters our egos, or that keeps us in our comfort zones. But when we remain neutral to the events of life, we expand our capacity for wisdom, selflessness, empathy, and love.

For example, let's say you are let go from your job because the company you work for is downsizing and your services are not considered essential. Suddenly, you can only see the ways in which you've been traumatized and can only experience the situation as a loss. Not only that, but you put yourself at the center of the drama. In your mind, this becomes a truly terrible event and you curse the company for letting you go, your old boss, and the people who continue to work there. You stay up all night going over and over what you could have done differently, what you should have said, what you can do to get back at them. You are so upset that you find it hard to focus on getting a new job, and you complain to everyone you know about how awful this is for you. You get angry at your friends because they seem unsympathetic and start avoiding them. In short, you are caught up in a huge drama, mostly of your own making.

By contrast, if you remain neutral, you leave yourself open to the huge range of possibilities life has to offer. In fact, the truth is that this may have been the best thing to happen to you in a long time. You often complained that the job was boring and you didn't feel much kinship with the people there. Now you are free to find something fresh and new that may be much more interesting and may even pay better. But as long as the drama is having its way with you, you just can't see the big picture. In a word, you need some *neutrality* to move forward.

The word "neutral" can evoke images of dullness, indifference, or even abnegation of responsibility, as in the case of an authority figure who refuses to intervene even in a clear-cut case of domestic violence. This is not the kind of neutrality I'm talking about here. The neutrality I'm talking about is the ability to recognize when you've gotten pulled into a self-centered drama and momentarily allowed your ego to take the wheel. You can tell this has happened when you feel contracted, over-activated, and anxious about the outcome of a certain situation, or when you are very concerned about how a particular event will affect you personally.

Conversely, returning to neutral is accompanied by feelings of expansion, acceptance, and calm. It feels good—like catching a wave instead of fighting the current. When you're in neutral, your heart is soft and your mind is unencumbered by fears and judgments. You become an open channel through which life can flow without resistance.

This wide-open state is the ideal basis from which to conduct any kind of spiritual practice. Just as an instrument will make more beautiful music when it's in tune, your prayers, meditations, ceremonies, and other spiritual work will be more effective when they come from a place of neutrality. From a shamanic point of view, there is nothing more important than remaining neutral, especially when doing shamanic work. Identifying with other people's woes or the drama that seems to be unfolding around them is a terrible idea. Feeling their pain renders you useless to help.

Sympathy can be deadly for all involved. But compassion and empathy are another story, and shamans readily cultivate these. Another way to put this is that matching other people's pain body or vibrations is never advisable. Neutrality allows you to function and help them with their needs. Shamans or healers who want to become part of the drama are generally ineffective. First of all, it robs patients of their experience, because it pulls the attention to the healer instead. Moreover, needing to help is the wrong motivation. Needing to help subtly contributes to the drama. On the other hand, wanting to be of service is a totally different motivation that is based on a neutral and stable offer to use a set of healing skills that may be needed or called for.

In the world of martial arts, an angry fighter is extremely vulnerable. Anger is an energy leak, a private drama that distracts the fighter. By the same token, fighters who are fearful are also vulnerable, because they are distracted by their concern that they may be hurt or killed. But fighters who have no agenda, who have no fear, who have nothing to lose and are totally neutral are the ones who win, because they have no drama-driven energy leaks.

Tibetan Buddhists, the *paqos* among the Qero of the Andes, Taoist masters of China, and Zen masters of Korea and Japan are experts at neutrality and actively cultivate it. Therefore, they are often considered among the world's most skilled teachers.

Neutrality is so important that I've included not one but four simple practices to help you establish this state of being. Although each one takes only a few seconds, each is highly effective at gently loosening the grip of the ego and returning you to a state of selflessness and benevolence.

Practice: Correct Neutral Now

Everybody gets upset, sad, angry, resentful, anxious, or agitated at one point or another. This technique allows you to reset quickly and return to neutrality.

1. The next time you realize you've become emotionally reactive or developed a strong opinion or preference about the events in your life, hold one hand vertically centered in front of your chest, with your thumb against your chest.

2. Silently issue yourself the command: "Correct neutral now."

3. Breathe deeply, and feel yourself returning to a calm, clear, objective state.

This practice helps you to realize that, sometimes, all it takes to return to neutral is to acknowledge that you've been knocked off-balance and set the intention to return.

Practice: Oh, Is That So?

There is a famous story about a Zen master who lived in a monastery near a small village and had many students. Everyone praised him as a great master, to which he replied only: "Oh, is that so?" One day, a village couple discovered that their teenage daughter was pregnant, and the girl named the master as the father. When they confronted him and accused him of being a terrible man, all he said was: "Oh, is that so?" The scandal caused the master to lose his reputation and his status. When the baby was born, the girl's parents gave her to the master to raise, and he accepted this task without complaint.

One year later, the guilt-ridden girl confessed that the baby's father was, in fact, a young fishmonger. She and her parents came to ask the master to return the child. Although by this point he had bonded with the infant, he gave her back without undue drama. The people of the village all praised him and told him he was a great master, to which he again replied only: "Oh, is that so?" He remained neutral even while being confronted alternately with praise and false accusations, when given unfair tasks, and when asked to part with that which was dear to him. Of course, he was a master. If you can achieve even a small amount of his neutrality, you are a very strong practitioner indeed!

You can draw on this master's wisdom to return to a neutral mind when you have been triggered or find yourself on some side of a polarity. As soon as you realize you've been triggered, focus on what your chattering mind is telling you and simply ask the question: "Oh, is that so?" This neutral contemplative statement takes no sides and passes no judgments. When you say it to yourself, you are neither agreeing with your mental chatter, nor offering it any resistance. When, like the master, you allow the energy of judgment to arise and pass, you soon find yourself at neutral again.

Practice: What If?

Often, when we are triggered by something, our minds begin to generate dire predictions: "She's going to be late, and we're going to miss the boat and end up sleeping on the sidewalk!" Rarely do we spend as much time contemplating the possibility of positive outcomes as we do worrying about negative ones, especially if we are already in a state of anxiety. This practice can help you correct this very common imbalance.

1. The next time you find yourself feeling stressed or triggered, ask yourself: "What if I were to discover a very simple solution to this problem?" Or "What if conditions outside of my control were to change so that this wasn't a problem anymore?" Or "What if instead of not knowing what to do, I were to discover that I intuitively know exactly what to do?"

2. Notice if the simple act of asking these question reduces your anxiety and broadens your perspective.

You can come up with your own variations on these questions. Use whichever words help you break out of your tunnel vision and remind you that while your mind's fear-based predictions may be the loudest, they aren't necessarily the most accurate.

Practice: Keep Don't Know Mind

In my thirties, I studied with a Korean Zen master whose English was poor, although his knowledge was great. He managed to condense the essence of Buddhism into four phrases: "Too many thinking," "Put it all down," "Only go straight," and "Keep don't know mind." These four phrases together comprise an essential understanding among Buddhists—the need to keep the mind silent and simply *know*.

We are often under the delusion that we need to know everything in order to function. We then demand of ourselves that we know what to do or understand immediately, no matter what confronts us. This usually only confounds us and makes us more confused and anxious. Buddhists, on the other hand, teach that the secret is to *not know*. It's okay not to know, even natural not to know, especially in shamanic work. We constantly face mystery, the unknown. What we know is based on what happened yesterday, not what is happening now. We are designed as curious, interested beings with a need to find out. So, if we admit that we don't know, that is actually perfectly okay.

Most of us don't know what we are doing most of the time. But great leaders *know* that they don't know, so they are curious and they contemplate the right questions. And then they realize that they know the next step to take. Knowing reveals itself; it is not necessarily acquired like data. Tibetan Buddhist master Tulku Urguen Rinpoche once said as much when he was asked by his students how he could be the right-hand man of the Dalai Lama when he kept his mind empty. He replied that it was easy: "I operate from knowing, not thinking."

The following principles can lead to a very neutral strategy for problem-solving that can result in a knowledge of how to proceed—and to awakening.

- Triggering situations result in "too many thinking."

- The best response is: "I don't know. I don't have to know. I'm putting it all down. I'm keeping don't know mind."

- When you admit to knowing nothing, but maintain curiosity, you stay humble. You "only go straight."

- When you are quiet, interested, reflective, observing, and listening, you are taking on the role of the curious student. You continue to "only go straight."

- When you recognize that some questions have arisen, you become the student and continue to "only go straight."

- When you listen quietly for answers, you connect with the teacher within or without. You "keep don't know mind."

That is how the quantum field functions as well, providing information on an as-needed basis. All we need to do is ask the right questions, and this triggers the quantum field to release information and answers that lead us inexorably toward great truths.

The Extraordinary
Practice of Self-Hypnosis

When I was in my twenties, having recently graduated with a bachelor's degree in sociology, I began working for a psychologist who was studying a population of people applying for disability benefits. A big part of my job was to administer a variety of tests to subjects who were suffering from alcoholism and drug addiction, as well as subjects with brain damage. While I found the work interesting, it was also quite stressful, especially because my days began and ended with a long commute in heavy traffic.

To cope, I began to attend free self-hypnosis sessions led by a Jesuit priest. From him, I learned a variety of techniques to enter into an altered state of consciousness and give myself suggestions about releasing tension and stress. These techniques helped me relax and ground myself after my busy days. Learning the basics inspired me to go deeper into more advanced techniques, and I began to incorporate some of the methods taught by Milton Erickson, a well-known and innovative psychiatrist who advanced the field of hypnosis in the United States. It wasn't until years later that I learned that hypnosis has been used by shamans as a healing technique for thousands of years. For example, a shaman may use self-hypnosis to access deep levels of the subconscious, or assist others in reaching these same states.

Although the concept of hypnotizing yourself may sound intimidating or even silly, it's actually very straightforward and completely safe. In fact, some Western doctors now recommend self-hypnosis as an aid in quitting smoking or to help treat insomnia. When you become skilled at self-hypnosis, you can steer your mind and body in the direction you want them to go, becoming an expert captain of your own craft. Self-hypnosis can also help you to achieve the deep states of relaxation, clarity, and calm that prepare you to work effectively with the other practices in this book.

Practice: Countdown to Clarity

Read over these instructions once or twice before you begin so you can remember what to do, as you will have your eyes closed during the practice itself.

1. Find a comfortable place where you can sit without interruption for at least ten minutes.

Try to sit in an upright position if you can, because lying down can simply put you to sleep. If your intention is to fall asleep, however, you can lie down in your bed and eliminate the suggestions to be aware and awake. Just concentrate on the ones that direct you to relax and go deeper.

2. Close your eyes and breathe normally, in through the nose and out through the mouth. Count backward from ten to one very slowly.

3. After each number, give yourself a few suggestions. These are simple words that express the state of mind and body you hope to achieve—whether that's relaxation, focus, or inner peace. For example:

> *Ten*—down, deep, deep
>
> *Nine*—relax, down, down deeper
>
> *Eight*—focused, bright, clear
>
> *Seven*—down, deeper within, deep
>
> *Six*—bright, aware, focused
>
> *Five*—clear and awake
>
> *Four*—deep down, very relaxed, falling lower

Three—awake, aware, clear, and bright

Two—deeper within, down, going down

One—luminous, clear, bright, totally aware

This process is called *induction*. Note that processes like this become more powerful the more you do them, because you are training your body and mind to follow these commands. After a few times, your body will automatically begin to respond the second you start to count.

The suggestions you use need not be complete sentences. As you can see from the example above, they can be simple phrases or even single words. It's helpful to alternate between suggestions to relax and suggestions to maintain your focus and awareness, so that you do not fall asleep. After completing the simple countdown, you can move on to making suggestions that are more specific. For example: "I am feeling more motivated and inspired all the time." Or "My work flows effortlessly."

There are two ways to reverse the induction process and return to normal awareness. The first is to begin to count up from one to ten, and with each count reverse the process so that you are rising up rather than going down. Just breathe slowly in through your nose and out through your mouth and feel your mind and body responding to your suggestions. For example:

One—lifting up

Two—rising and lifting

Three—feeling my fingers and toes

Four—up higher

Five—awake, alert, aware

And so on to ten.

The second method is even simpler. Just count to four, snap your fingers, and mentally or verbally state the word: "Back!"

Practice: Overcoming Resistance

There are parts of ourselves that can be very stubborn, resistant, fearful, or even uncooperative. So giving yourself another option is a very important part of this practice. Try telling yourself that you don't have to do this, but that you might find it helpful. This allows those resistant parts of you to feel safer, not coerced. Most people do not like to feel compelled. They want to be invited. They want to feel free to choose. Getting that aspect's cooperation is very important. This is one of the great contributions of Erickson to the art of self-hypnosis.

To invoke this power of choice, you can use the generic induction technique described in the previous practice and then attach phases like these:

- I am becoming more productive in a good way every day.

- I am feeling more motivated and inspired all the time.

- I am effortlessly finding that I am producing better results.

- I don't have to do this. No one is making me do this.

- I just find it easier to get better results in everything I do.

- I could easily just go on the way I was. That would be very easy to do.

- I could stay the same or choose to adapt to changing circumstances.

- I can do whatever I want. Maybe I will take a different path here.

- I find I just want to be more effective in an effortless way.

- Getting more productive results is just easier.

- No one is forcing me to do this. I am free, after all.

Practice: Going Deeper

Here is a little more advanced induction technique based in Ericksonian principles that you can use for a variety of purposes—to give yourself positive suggestions, to acquire new good habits, and to heal yourself on various levels. It is quite powerful and effective.

1. Begin by sitting erect if you want to remain awake or lying down if you want to relax and fall asleep. You may want to record your own voice guiding you through the statements below. If not, you can just speak them from memory.

2. If you are using the phrases below, use the pronoun "you" instead of "I." In this practice, one part of you is issuing suggestions to another part of you. Note that it does not use the earlier counting method, but a different approach to guide you.

   • Relax and go deeper.

   • There is an invisible force that, normally, you pay no attention to.

   • This force is amazingly strong.

   • Focus your attention on your body for a moment and notice the effect of gravity upon it.

- Gravity is always there, but you don't often notice it. It is pulling you down with great force.

- You can feel it on your body, pulling you down.

- Feel it on the back of your head, your back, your pelvis, where your arms are resting, the backs of your legs (or the bottoms of your feet).

- You can feel it where your clothes are clinging to your skin.

- You could resist gravity. No one is making you lie (sit) there. You are free.

- You could fight it and try to get up. That is okay. But that would take a lot of effort. You would have to work against it.

- Or you could relax into it and let gravity do what it does. It won't hurt you. It is keeping your body from floating away. Your body is safely parked for now. It won't be going anywhere.

- While gravity is having a great impact on your body, notice that it has no impact on your thoughts and feelings. No impact on your imagination.

+ You can go anywhere you want, think whatever you wish. You are free, free, free. Free as a bird flying.

3. Here you can begin making your suggestions. When you are ready to return to an ordinary state of awareness, simply use the techniques you learned in the first practice.

This is a great induction method for a number of shamanic practices. For example, you can use it to prepare to journey into a cave and follow deeper passageways to find the answers to a question, or to visit a guide or wise older person, perhaps a spiritual teacher who will advise you on a matter of concern. Or you can use it to enlist the assistance of a power animal or ally regarding some matter.

PART TWO

Energetic Practices

From a shamanic perspective, life is all about energy—acquiring it, spending it, sharing it, and allowing it to move from one place to another, changing form as it goes. Indeed, you could say that most of the challenges in life boil down to the ways we consciously or unconsciously try to resist this never-ending flow. The practices in this section are all about helping you work with energy—putting it to its highest use, releasing it from the places it's gotten stuck, and redirecting it where you want it to go. Most of us are vulnerable to "energy leaks" from time to time, and these practices help you to plug those leaks quickly so you can gain the vitality you need to reach your highest aspirations.

The Extraordinary Practice
of Clearing Addictions

Back when smartphones first came into use, I was a big fan of the technology. As a scholar, I like to keep abreast of world news. These new devices let me read the news anywhere, anytime. How convenient!

Before I knew it, I was scrolling through news feeds multiple times a day, lost in a never-ending sea of information. I felt as if I had to have the latest updates on any number of different stories. It was no longer enough to read the morning paper, then go about the rest of my day. If I hadn't checked the news on my phone in more than an hour or two, I felt restless and irritable. Not only that, but my brain soon became tired from processing this flood of information, most of which was pretty depressing. Even though reading the news left me feeling unsatisfied and anxious, I tried to alleviate those feelings by reading even more of it! You could say I had a greed for news that was becoming self-destructive.

I soon realized that I had become trapped in an addiction spiral. Because I still needed to be informed of world events for my work, I signed up for a weekly e-mail news summary, and read it carefully instead of mindlessly scrolling through reports on my phone whenever I had an idle moment. I also began to work with a powerful Toltec exercise for ending addiction, which I share with you below. Before long, the energy that had been draining out of me as a result of my scrolling had been replenished, and I felt back to my usual vibrant self.

Let's face it. Almost all of us are addicted to something, to some degree—except perhaps a few self-realized souls who have moved completely beyond addiction. Even if you are free from the "major" addictions like alcohol or drugs, you may still crave attention, wealth, sex, or endless stimulation. Although these cravings may not amount to a medical problem, they are still addictions in the sense that you may spend a great deal of your time and energy pursuing them, whether or not they are good for you, and whether or not they provide you with any lasting satisfaction. They are all forms of subconscious greed.

Most of us do not want to examine our addictions. Instead, we surrender to the cycle of pursuit, temporary fulfillment, and the reappearance of the original craving or some variation of it. Even when we know that acquiring the object of our addiction won't satisfy us for long, we still chase it, resigning ourselves to the disappointment that will inevitably ensue.

In Buddhism, this cycle is thought to lie at the root of all suffering. The Buddha taught that humans suffer because we continually strive for things that are impermanent and therefore cannot provide lasting satisfaction. New possessions lose their novelty and eventually wear out; relationships begin to challenge us when the fantasy fades; praise and recognition fade away, leaving us hungry for the next achievement; the pleasure of food, sex, and drugs reaches its peak, then begins to decline. Instead of recognizing that the momentary bliss we experience when we acquire the object of our desire is our true nature, we believe that this bliss has something to do with acquiring the object—so we search for it again and again.

In my experience, the key to overcoming addiction is to realize once and for all that the bliss you feel has nothing to do with getting the object of your craving, and everything to do with being fully present, without ego or suffering. Once you start to cultivate that state of presence on an ongoing basis, life itself becomes blissful. You can access those feelings of satisfaction and non-craving at any time—you no longer need the drug, the drink, the praise, or whatever you're addicted to, in order to experience them briefly. The alternative to despair and suffering is realizing that you already have access to whatever you crave—you've simply been making an error of perception that gave rise to your addiction. That craving, by the way, is always for love, and love is already present. It's just that we ignore it and think it lies elsewhere. The two practices below are very effective at bringing about this realization.

Both of these practices allow you to step back and do something other than obsess fruitlessly about your helplessness in the face of addiction. They are proactive, even if you are only observing the process of the addiction. They give you an organized and focused method for addressing something that thrives on chaos, confusion, and denial in order to survive. While they won't necessarily produce instantaneous results, they engender an immediate feeling of progress and will soon lessen the grip the addiction has on you.

That is the key—to break the stranglehold the addiction has on you so that, with discipline, you can ultimately free yourself. This is not unlike untying a knot in a rope. The first loosening of the tangle is the most challenging. It goes without saying that you should expect some resistance from the addiction in the face of your attempt to dislodge it. Pay it no mind whatsoever.

Practice: Observing Your Addiction

This first practice helps you to bring mindfulness to your addictions so that you can correct your perceptions about what you really crave—love.

1. Select a mild addiction—something small and manageable. Do not start with a very severe addiction if you have one, because you may have a deep belief that overcoming it is impossible, which can make it more difficult for this practice to work.

2. Contemplate the addiction. When do the cravings arise? Do they come up when you are stressed? Sad? Bored? What are the triggers in your environment that nudge you toward your addiction? What sensations do you feel in your body when you become aware of the cravings?

3. The next time your addiction arises, watch it closely as it unfolds in real time. Observe it; witness it working. Notice how it plays out without judgment, without blame, without evaluation. What emotions come up for you? Do you feel guilt? Shame? Resistance? Or a thrill of rebellion and self-justification? Do you feel stressed

and unloved? Do you feel that the pleasure you seek is like having a lover love you?

4. Let yourself experience these reactions on a sensory level. In other words, try to get past your thoughts and into your physical feelings. Do you feel sweaty? Tense? Do you experience a sense of inner pressure? How closely can you attend to these feelings without escaping back into your thoughts?

5. If you allow yourself to have the object of your addiction, do you notice a feeling of relief? What does this feel like at a sensory level? Does it feel as good as you imagined? Or can you feel the seeds of the next craving already beginning to sprout?

6. Repeat this practice as often as you are able. The more closely you can attend to your feelings at a sensory level, the less power your addiction will have over you and the more clearly you will see the truth of the cycle.

This is the practice in a nutshell. But now let's look at the process in a little more detail to make it real for you.

As you go through the steps of the practice, step back and observe any shame or guilt you may begin to feel. Consider that the shame or guilt only compounds the problem because it raises your stress level, making you want relief even more. Perhaps you feel you must rush to commit the act that will bring you relief before the guilt gets too strong or the shame unbearable. Perhaps the feeling of being "bad" somehow activates your desire to rebel and do it anyway. After all, nobody should be able to tell you what you can or can't do. But this sense of resistance can become a justification to engage in your addictive process.

Notice the ramping up of your craving. You can't seem to get it out of your mind. You need some relief. You seem to be past the point of self-control or distracting yourself away from it. You are committed to your addiction at this point, like a worshipper at the feet of a golden idol. Perhaps the addiction involves some simple pleasure—watching porn, shopping online, scratching an itch, looking at social media, or playing video games. Or perhaps it actually involves pain—picking scabs, pulling at your hair, biting your nails, or cutting your skin. In a way, it does not matter whether what you are seeking is pain or pleasure, because it is all hooked up with getting relief from a craving. It engages you in drama. It makes you feel alive again.

Now consider this. Let's say you succumb to your addiction and engage in the forbidden behavior. This may involve many emotions—shame or guilt for spending money or time on this behavior; the worry that your addiction is getting worse or harming you in some way; fierce recriminations that beat you up from within; satisfaction at the pleasure of rebelling; anger at the world; sadness over your plight, and so on. Notice that all these feelings are familiar; you have experienced them so many times before. Nothing's changed; nothing's new. There are no amazing insights, just repetition.

Observe how the feeling of relief surges as you satisfy your craving, how you suddenly relax and don't care anymore. Look closely, because this may last only a very short time before the craving comes back. What is occurring here? Do you attribute this momentary relief to the attainment of the object of your desire? Do you actually believe that the object is responsible for your relief and is absolutely necessary? Or perhaps to feel neutral again? Or perhaps even to feel somewhat elevated again?

This is a very important moment—the moment when the lie is perpetuated and even strengthened. I say lie because you *know* that these feelings are false. You *know* that the object of your desire will never, ever satisfy you permanently. Perhaps you don't even want that to be true. Why? Because if you admit the truth, the game begins to unravel. And you worry that, if it unravels, you will ultimately lose the object you believe is responsible for your relief. And heavens, you can't live without that! Or can you?

And this is where the heavy lifting comes in. When you obtain the sacred object of your craving—the sugary dessert, the ripped off scab, the chunk of hair, the scratched itch, the ejaculation, the money spent, the game played—you feel relief, because your craving is temporarily ended and the agitation it causes is at the root of your suffering, despite all your attempts to deny it.

But here is the unvarnished truth: *The addiction is actually the suffering itself.* And you are addicted to suffering and addicted to not suffering all at the same time. It's crazy, but true. Moreover, if you have an addiction, you *know* this is true, whether you want to admit it or not. All addictions behave the same way.

So what happens when you lose your craving—even if only momentarily? You are returned to a state of "not craving." And this state is actually your true state, your natural state, your state without ego, without suffering. For a few minutes, you are just *being*, just present, just conscious of your aliveness, and this is so nice. You think that this state has something to do with your addictive behavior, with attaining the object of your desire. But it doesn't. That is a false belief in a false cause. The two actually have nothing to do with each other.

Your natural state is always there, always present at some level. Think of a diamond that is covered with dust. When you scrape off the dust, you reveal the precious gem beneath. But the diamond was always there. It didn't go anywhere; it didn't disappear from reality. It was always there under the dirt. And just like the diamond, your natural state, your alive presence, is perpetual and infinite. It's just that when your craving stops, even for just a few seconds, you notice it.

So in some ways, your addiction may be your savior. I am not insinuating that relief is somehow Nirvana. But it can be the first step in a process of enlightenment, the relief of suffering. It can unlock the door. The door has yet to swing open all the way—that comes later. But this process of unlocking the door and swinging it open is vastly simplified when you actually understand what lurks beneath the surface of your addictive behavior—a lie that must be exposed. This is where the potential for awakening dwells, although distorted through dysfunctional behaviors that we all share. It's no one's fault. But it is everyone's responsibility to understand this. This awakening may happen all at once, or it may happen gradually. But it will happen.

We as human beings are on the grand adventure of awakening to what has always already been true—that we are multidimensional beings of unimaginable power and presence, and we are only pretending to be in this tiny little experiment of being physically based humans. Our true nature is that we are all expressions of Spirit; at our core is love, beauty, unfathomable intelligence, and presence. We are not limited by either time or space.

Now here is the part that may be hard to accept because of our conditioning. Whatever we do, whatever we are, is all within the presence of Spirit, or God for those of you who prefer that term. Even during the process of engaging in our addictions, we are expressing our divine selves. How can that be? Because there is nothing but Spirit. Ever. Anywhere. Spirit is everywhere all the time. Are there any exceptions? No. Everything else is an imagined game.

The monkey mind is crowded with endless thoughts. But thinking is a gift that only works if it is used in the service of the gifts that Spirit has given us. Thinking can help to free us, but it is like a map. No matter how much we want to believe it is the territory itself, it is not. It is just thought, and thoughts are an endless river that can confuse as well as enlighten.

Addictions are nothing more than confused thoughts passing through a house of mirrors. Eventually, we will all find our way out. We can take as long as we want. It is time for humanity to come to terms with the gargantuan lie that external objects will provide permanent peace and happiness. They won't. Ever. The lesson is clear. And liberation lies in our clarity. Objects are nothing. What we need, we already have. You cannot pretend to know this. You have to perceive it with clarity. Hopefully, this practice and the realizations you can gain from self-observation will make the task easier for you.

So that is the core of the practice. Now, here are the rules of the game. And when you know the rules, you can win.

- Addictive thinking seeks to relieve stress, but actually causes more stress.

- Addictions seek to find relief from stress by finding an object on which to fixate, to crave, and then to obtain.

- These objects may be perceptions, thoughts, sensations, or images.

- Obtaining the object of your desire does not produce happiness.

- Obtaining the object of your desire does stop the craving for a short time, revealing a peek at an underlying natural state of peace that is always present, but obscured by distractions.

- Seeing the absolute truth of this fact can lead to a dismantling of the addictive behavior.

- Realizing this may temporarily cause overwhelming despair.

- The alternative to despair and suffering is realizing that you already have access to what you actually crave—the cessation of your suffering and the recognition of what is actually true. The joy and beauty of your being, your presence, your awareness that you are alive—this is present right now in everyone, including you. It has just been obscured by confused thought.

If you want to make rapid progress, read these rules several times a day. A small investment of your time at the cost of your suffering will be your reward. This is guaranteed to transform your life.

Practice: Starving Your Addiction

This is an ancient Toltec practice aimed at starving and eliminating your addictions. The Toltecs called this the "transform pleasure process," although the name is slightly misleading because no addictions are actually pleasurable. What they really meant was that all addictions are trying to ward off stress and, in that sense, they can lead to a temporary relief of pain or anxiety. Ultimately, the purpose of the practice is to redirect energy leaks in your life.

Sometimes pleasures are addictions that bring gratification—eating too much, drinking alcohol, smoking, taking pills, or engaging in other lustful behaviors that are addictive or harmful to yourself or others. Sometimes these addictions are not apparently pleasurable, but provide some avenue of relief—workaholism, bulimia, anorexia, whining or complaining all the time, getting others to be annoyed or angry with you, needing to be right all the time, demanding everyone's attention all the time, needing to dominate and control everyone, and so on. This practice can help you to redirect the energy wasted on these behaviors toward more constructive goals.

1. This practice is best done standing, but that is not required. Stand with your legs apart for stability and cup your hands just below your genitals. Accuracy in positioning is very important to the Toltecs. Take three deep breaths and, on the first out breath, release any heavy energy you are feeling. With your second out breath, feel yourself coming into alignment with the rhythm of the universe. With your third, set an intention to align yourself with the current position of the sun, moon, and planets wherever they are.

2. Select your major issue or addiction—in other words, your biggest energy leak.

3. Call in the energy of that addiction. To do this, you can shake a rattle or imagine one and make a verbal statement like: "I call in the energy of my sugar addiction." As you rattle, call out the Nahuatl word for "come": *Shewalway, shewalway, shewalway.*

4. Imagine yourself filling your cupped hands with the energy that usually goes into gratifying yourself with the object of your addiction. Pull this energy from various parts of your body while breathing deeply in and out, coughing, grunting, and doing whatever else you need to do to get this energy to move. Remember that if you do not involve your breath, you will accomplish little here. So even if you feel foolish or self-conscious, breathe in and out deeply. Especially concentrate on the joints of your body where your various bones come together, like the discs between your vertebrae. This is where energy becomes trapped and needs to be released.

5. When you determine the cup is full, pour some of this energy into your navel to support your highest destiny, abundance, and prosperity.

6. Move the cup up to your chest and pour some into your heart to support inner flowering.

7. Raise the cup to your throat and pour some in there to support your strength, power, and discipline, and to strengthen your will and grow your perseverance to change the pattern.

8. Raise the cup to your brow or Third Eye and pour the rest of the energy in there to feed your clarity, joy, and vision. Use the reassigned energy to pursue your highest endeavors.

9. Repeat this process three times, then release your hands and give yourself a good shake.

10. Join your hands together and say *Ometeotle,* the Toltec word for "You are complete."

Repeat this process daily for a week and see what happens. If you have a severe addiction, you should seek professional help. If you have a pretty good handle on your addictions, you can simply do the practice periodically as needed.

Once you are familiar with this practice, it should take you no more than ten or fifteen minutes to do. That is a very short investment of time to clear a scourge or many demons from your life.

The Extraordinary
Practice of Clearing
Through Duplication

When I was in my late twenties, I studied with a spiritual teacher who was a clairvoyant—a person who can see auras and energy fields—and he knew a wide range of practices for clearing trauma and balancing energy. The practice I found most effective was called "duplication," which consisted of overwriting traumatic memories with newer versions, until all the emotional charge had been drained out. Later, I encountered similar versions of this trauma-clearing technique in other spiritual traditions, including Toltec shamanism and Zen Buddhism. Tibetans derived a powerful set of techniques from Bon, an ancient shamanic tradition that predated their conversion to Buddhism. They used it to help clear their minds of distracting thoughts and memories during deep meditation.

Most of us have at least a handful of painful memories whose emotional charge we can't quite shake.

These memories of rejection, betrayal, humiliation, or abuse live in our bodies and minds, draining our energy in subtle or not-so-subtle ways. If the pain attached to them is raw enough, we can even find ourselves withdrawing from anything in life that reminds us of the event that wounded us in the past. If we were hurt by a group of friends, we may avoid all relationships; if we were humiliated at work, we may stop sticking our necks out and sharing ideas. This withdrawal can cause life to get smaller and smaller, as we retreat into a cage of self-protection.

Although it may feel safe to live within the confines of this cage, we are never truly free of the pain. Indeed, instead of being a short and temporally limited event, the original rejection or humiliation now controls our entire lives—hardly an improvement! By facing the painful feelings in a safe and careful way, however, we can reduce their grip on us and begin to participate fully in life instead of hiding in our self-imposed cage.

Fortunately, there is a very simple method of erasing the trauma of our original memories and any subsequent memories that have become attached to them. This method consists of mentally "duplicating" the original memory until you have successfully overwritten the painful version, replacing it with a memory that is free of emotional charge. When you intentionally invoke a painful memory, and willingly experience the feelings associated with it, you automatically begin to reduce its power over you. It's a little bit like choosing to face a fear like swimming in deep water or public speaking. When you choose to engage with what you fear, you assume a position of strength.

Practice: Overwriting Traumatic Memories

This practice can teach you to handle the painful feelings associated with your traumatic memories, thereby lessening their hold on you. With enough repetition, it can drain away all the negative charge associated with the memories. Over the years, I have taught this technique to many students and those who use it regularly has always found it very gratifying.

1. Identify a traumatic memory you would like to address. The practice is more effective if you still feel stress when you recall it.

2. Recall everything about it you can—the sounds, smells, sights, and feelings you experienced during the event.

3. As you allow yourself to feel these things fully, notice if they flare up and then diminish in intensity, like coals burning themselves out. You may find that the memory morphs into a symbol or facsimile, and that is okay.

4. Get creative. Ask yourself some subjective questions. What color is it? What temperature? What are its characteristics? Hard or soft? Old or new? Sharp or dull? How big does it seem? Huge or tiny? In between?

5. When you have remembered everything you can, imagine you have a photocopier. Place your memory or symbol of it as it exists at this moment into the photocopier and make an exact copy of it.

6. Visualize yourself inserting the copy into the original so that it disappears into it. It is not just superimposed on the original. It is no longer a separate thing. It is, in fact, exactly the same as the original and can occupy the same space that the original does. They become one thing. Take a moment and observe the results.

7. Does this new, updated version of your memory feel a little less intense than the original? If not, this is perfectly okay. Just repeat the process.

8. If you do notice a reduction in intensity, describe what has changed. How is it different in terms of feeling? What are the changes in the image? Is it smaller? Cooler? More blue or red? Is there more or less anger? More or less fear? Are you more relaxed?

9. Repeat the process, this time introducing the changes you noticed. Insert your new copy into the latest version of the memory. In other words, you are always inserting the latest copy into the latest version. You are never going back to the original version that you started with.

10. Continue modifying the feelings and imagery with subsequent versions until you've arrived at a place of neutrality. This means that you can still recall the event, but without any charge or triggered reaction.

To achieve complete neutrality for particularly challenging traumas that may have taken place over many years, you may have to do this many times. Like all processes, this practice will give you greater mastery and confidence in the results. I find it useful to do a very quick version in just a few moments when I am on the run. And keep in mind that if you combine this technique with asking allies for help, you will double its effectiveness.

The Extraordinary Practice of Dissolving Fear

The greatest obstacle to spiritual transformation is fear. Fear is so central to the source of human suffering that I am devoting extra space to it here to help you understand what is involved in dissolving it.

Several years ago, my daughter and I took a trip to Guatemala. One night, we went out for dinner, and when we returned to our hotel we found that our room had been ransacked. Our cell phones, camera equipment, and money were all missing. As if that weren't bad enough, when we reported the theft to the hotel manager, his mood quickly changed from sympathetic and helpful to paranoid and threatening. Throughout the ordeal, I watched my mind and body going through all kinds of reactions, from fear and panic to anger and even amusement. My thoughts were filled with worry. What if the hotel manager was in league with the thieves, and he extorted even more money from us? What if he accused us of faking the theft and had us thrown in jail? I imagined us trapped in a Guatemalan jail with no way to call for help. Unlikely, but given the fraught and unpredictable way the hotel manager was acting, who knew?

Luckily, my decades of spiritual training had prepared me well to deal with fear. Instead of spinning off into panic, doing and saying things that would only make the situation worse, I stayed calm and kept a sense of humor, watching my mind's gymnastics with gentle compassion. My daughter and I remained perfectly safe and enjoyed the rest of our trip, even if we didn't get to take as many pictures as we'd planned.

Indigenous peoples around the world agree that there are two fundamental fears that all human beings experience. The first is the fear of abandonment—being rejected, separated, or exiled. So great is our fear of abandonment that some will even commit suicide after being rejected by a love interest, their family, or their community. The second universal fear is the terror of being imprisoned, enslaved, or entrapped. Many will kill themselves to avoid the consequences of going to jail or becoming a slave.

To understand the source of these two fears, we need look no further than a fetus's experience of the womb. Despite the fact that this environment is the nurturing nest and incubator for the fetus, it is also the breeding ground of the two great fears. The womb is so nurturing that the developing fetus does not want to be expelled from it, and this is associated with the fear of abandonment. But the fetus is also growing ever larger and knows that it must eventually leave the womb or die within its tight confines. This predicament is associated with the fear of entrapment. According to the indigenous peoples I've studied with, these fears are part of human nature—challenges that we become stronger by mastering.

Beneath the umbrella of these two basic fears, all the other fears proliferate. For example, the basic fear of abandonment gives rise to fear of being judged by others, of not being good enough, of failure and humiliation, and of losing the people we love. The basic fear of entrapment engenders the fear of being smothered in our intimate relationships, or trapped in a job or a marriage, or restricted somehow by others' demands and needs. If you really think about it, even very concrete fears like getting lost in the woods or spiders can be traced back to these two basic fears!

These two great fears, entrapment and abandonment, break down into sub-fears that have been known by a number of names in different traditions—demons, dark spirits, obstacles, fear patterns, sins, or the work of the devil. In shamanic cultures, they are often seen as parasites. What you believe about the origin of these fears matters, however, because you either feel victimized and helpless in the face of them or empowered to confront them, handle them, and erase them. If you believe they are caused by external forces, you will be more inclined to enlist the aid of a priest or shaman to fight them off for you. If you understand that they are part of the challenges every human being faces as a result of internal forces, then you may be more inclined to view them with sobriety and courage, and reframe them as manageable through personal discipline and work on yourself. These different ways of reacting to fear have much to do with your spiritual and psychological maturity.

No matter how we categorize our fears, however, the key to overcoming them is *observation*. In physics, this is called the "observer effect"—a phenomenon in which the mere existence of an observer can alter the behavior of the thing being observed. When we try to ignore or suppress our fears, they grow stronger and stronger. But when we saturate them with our awareness, they begin to weaken and dissolve.

Fear Patterns

Our fears tend to feed into several kinds of negative behaviors known as fear patterns. The fear of abandonment most often results in self-destruction, greed, self-deprecation, and arrogance. The fear of entrapment more often results in martyrdom, impatience, and stubbornness. These behaviors have a way of drawing to you the very situations of which you are most afraid. That is how greedy people end up with nothing and arrogant people end up humiliated. Even more nasty is the fact that these behaviors cause you to do to yourself and others what you are most afraid might happen to you. Thus someone who is arrogant and fears being criticized will mercilessly criticize themselves and others.

These behaviors are obstacles to manifesting your most productive self—as the Toltecs say, manifesting your greatest destiny. Moreover, they further neutralize your efforts to attain your goals in life. You will not be happy as long as you are ruled by these patterns.

These fear patterns have remained unchanged throughout history and across cultures. Shakespeare remains popular centuries after he lived because he captured the essence of them in his stories and characters. Religious and spiritual teachers have railed against them since the dawn of time, yet they persist in the human race like the cloying odor of death. No one appears to be immune to them, and even the most saintly or advanced humans have to guard against them or inevitably succumb to them. There are so many stories of gurus, cult leaders, and clergy who have been brought down by one or another of these behaviors. What is so interesting about them is that we tend to be embarrassingly blind to our own fear-based behaviors, but can readily see them in others. And this means that others can readily see ours as well.

While these patterns are exceptionally detrimental to life, they can also be valuable guides to what *not* to do. They teach the hard way and pose challenges, which, if overcome, result in great strength of character.

The Game of Life

In order to truly understand fear patterns, it can be helpful to think of life as a game. Winning the game means being happy, satisfied, and successful at meeting your goals. Losing means being miserable and failing to meet your goals. Think of fear patterns as the opposing team trying to defeat you at all costs. To win, you must be aware of your goal, aware of the opposing team's strategies to defeat you, and aware of strategies to erase the threat your opponents present. That is not enough, however. You must also be skilled enough and powerful enough to defeat the other team. In order to be powerful enough, you have to eliminate your energy leaks and be able to accumulate enough power and energy to overcome them.

Fear patterns are excellent at robbing you of your power and energy so that they can overcome you and defeat you in a weakened state. One of the main ways they do that is to seduce you into not taking responsibility for your life. This weakens you very quickly.

Another way they trap you is to get you to identify with your fears so that you think they are real. This puts you into a state of resistance and, once there, you are easy to defeat because you waste your energy on defending yourself and resisting your fear. You cannot afford to let them do that to you.

To win the game, you must get into shape. In general, your best bet is to take full responsibility for what happens in your life, even when that is difficult and situations don't seem to be your fault. This is the power position. The next step is to stop identifying with your fears. You must be able to say—and mean: "I have some fears, but I am not my fears." The truth is, you are *never* your fears. Never were, never will be.

I often tell my students that if they are feeling awful they are in the grip of their fear patterns. Whatever they are struggling with is not who they are. The natural condition for a human being is to feel great. You need to believe that and strive for it. But you will never feel great if you think you are flawed.

Unmasking Fear

So where do most fears originate? The answer is simple. Fear comes from a feeling of being isolated and disconnected from others, from yourself, and from your source. Even the fear of entrapment originates in isolation from others, and isolation leads to a lower chance of survival. All humans, and indeed other animals, respond to this feeling of separation with fear. Eventually this just confirms what they feared in the first place, and a vicious cycle begins. Remember: fear is an idea. It is part of your opponents' arsenal of tricks to defeat you. Engage in fear patterns and be defeated. Refuse and win the game of life. But to defeat your enemy, you must know your enemy. So now it is time to arm yourself with vital information.

There are actually many practices that can slowly eliminate fear patterns. Sometimes you need the help of a good therapist when they have gotten out of hand. The practice I recommend here is very simple, but very effective. It is based in *observation*. The key to understanding fear patterns is to recognize their desire to remain obscure, unnoticed, hiding in plain sight. These patterns are masters at appearing like rational responses to normal situations, but nothing could be further from the truth. They are defense mechanisms that are not really protective at all. In fact, they will deliver you into the maw of what you fear most. Anyone who thinks stubbornness or arrogance is a good response has a lot to learn. More often they are disastrous responses that create even more fear.

Here are some sobering facts about fear patterns:

+ If you resist these patterns, they only get stronger. What you resist persists.

+ If you ignore these patterns, they only get stronger.

+ If you judge them and attack them, they only get stronger.

+ If you feel shame and guilt about them, they only get stronger.

+ If you indulge them, they only get stronger.

Fears, just like viruses, have had hundreds of thousands of years to master their strategies to work against us. They are, as shamans say, "worthy opponents." But overcoming unworthy opponents doesn't make you strong. Overcoming worthy ones does.

Fear patterns have several weaknesses we can exploit to wipe them out. Each time we feel fearful, we engage in a single battle in an overall war about who will win the game of life—our fears or our courageous selves. Shamans consider every one of these battles a life-and-death struggle in the overall journey to become free. This means that you have to pay total attention to what is happening, just like a predator does when stalking its prey. Your fears are always stalking you. You need to turn the tables on them and stalk them instead. Every time you indulge your fears, you suffer an energy leak that weakens you, a result you cannot afford if your aim is to be free.

You need to know that you are *already* free, that your fear patterns are not stronger than your core self. Why? Because you are designed to win by nature. This idea is so important that I am going to repeat it here in a slightly different way. You are designed by nature to win. Therefore, you can't believe the lies that your fears tell you. Ever.

Notice that when you are observing something in yourself, you are at a bit of a distance from it. This means that you are not as identified with it from this point of view, and this is a key step in the strategy to outmaneuver it. The pattern has maximum power over you only when you are completely caught up in it, when you think that it "is" you. But when you step back and look at your fear, you see that perhaps it is not you after all, just another thing in the universe of so-called things—something you can choose to keep or reject, a bit like cleaning out your desk.

Maintaining this stance hour after hour, day after day is critical to your overall success at the game of life. Do not lose your neutrality. And if you do, bounce right back without any recrimination whatsoever.

Practice: Exposing Fear Patterns

Remember that fear patterns prefer keeping to the shadows where they will not be noticed. They hate having a light shining on them. So shine that light as often as you are able and do it soon. They will scuttle away. This practice can help you do that.

1. The next time you find yourself caught in the grips of fear, allow yourself to feel it as a pure sensation. Experience it without running from it. When predators track or stalk prey, they stay with it.

2. At first, your fear may feel very solid and hard. You may feel a strong sense of urgency to respond to it by taking some course of action that helps you avoid whatever it is that you fear. This is when the fear patterns strike. You may feel stubborn, impatient, victimized, critical, or beaten. Instead, try to stay with the direct experience of the fear. Avoid the distractions.

3. What would this experience be like if you hadn't labeled it with the word "fear"? If you had no access to language and could only experience the fear as a sensation in your body, would it still be frightening?

4. As you observe your fear, don't try to change it. Just notice if the mere fact of observing your fear causes it to change. Track these changes closely. Does your fear flare up, growing more intense in an effort to get control of you? Does it abate momentarily, flickering on and off like a candle? This is what one of my teachers described as "experiencing your experience." Experience it thoroughly. And when it vanishes, replace it with pure space.

5. Inspect your fear so closely that you can see every individual particle that composes it. Allow it to break up from a solid, unified mass into a swarm of completely neutral particles of energy that could come together as something entirely different. Another teacher explained it to me this way: Everything is composed of particles. To eliminate something, reduce it to individual particles and destroy its cohesiveness.

6. When you feel ready, re-dedicate the energy you recover to the service of your best and highest potential in this life.

The Extraordinary Practice of Opening and Closing Energy Fields

All around the world, different peoples have different names for the planes of existence that exist beyond our ordinary awareness. Shamans reference the Spirit World; ancient Hindus spoke of the Akasha; Taoists in China wrote of the Tao; and today, quantum physicists publish papers on the zero-point or quantum field.

Throughout history, the artwork and music of cultures around the world have touched on a set of universal themes. Experiences like falling in love, feeling betrayed, grieving a loss, or celebrating a victory have always resonated with most people. I like to think of these universal experiences as energy fields that have existed since the beginning of time, and into which most humans tap at one point or another. You can imagine them like the power grid in a city. The grid is always there, and anyone in the city can plug into it—or unplug from it—whenever they like.

Some believe that we can access various distinct fields that are common across human cultures. For example, one field might be the divine masculine, with attributes like generosity, protectiveness, and strength. It also carries the more negative attributes of violence, control, and aggression. Another field might be the divine feminine, with attributes of receptiveness, nurturing, and support, and its accompanying negative fields of chaos, voraciousness, and manipulation. Other fields or sets of frequencies might be related to beauty, clarity, connectedness, wisdom, playfulness, animals, plants, minerals, gems, wind, water, earth, and an almost infinite list of other qualities that we experience as human beings.

It would be tempting to think of these fields as a spectrum occupying higher and lower ranges in relation to each other, but that would not be exactly right. The truth is that these fields co-exist. They are nested together and equal in value. They do not form a progression with relative positions, although each is actually a set of vibrations that can be used either positively or negatively. Rather than think of vibrations that are put to negative purpose as "bad," however, it would be more accurate to say that using the frequencies negatively simply produces a different set of results—for example, more suffering and less joy than would result from using them positively.

Good hunters, animal trainers, horse whisperers, and animal researchers are all tuned in to the field of animals. Some, like Jane Goodall or Steve Irwin, are resonant with the fields of specific animals like chimpanzees or crocodiles. This resonance does not occur by accident, but is the result of focused collaboration with certain fields of reality, whether the person is conscious of it or not. This is what shamans call their "medicine." The same is true for fire-breathers, hydrologists, electricians, carpenters, metallurgists, nuclear physicists, meteorologists, zoologists, and oceanographers.

The Web of Life

Fields can work together or apart. The field of weather has rain, snow, sleet, wind, warmth, blazing heat, cold, calm, tempest, thunder, lightning, and humidity, as well as many other attributes. Obviously, these are related to other fields that have to do with water, air, fire, and earth. This is why the fields form an interwoven tapestry that works together in many combinations for our benefit. Shamans understand this and call it the web of life.

Weather shamans are those who can call up rain on demand, or direct the winds, or change a storm's direction. I have personally witnessed the effectiveness of the weather paqos in the Andes of Peru and have seen and experienced how they redirected storms so they did not disturb the special *despacho* fire ceremony they were conducting for us. Weather shamanism is a specialty practiced all over the world. Once shamans open the field and go into resonance with it, they *become* the rain and can command it to do their bidding. But in order to become the weather, you have to let go of personal agendas and that takes a lot of personal discipline.

How can shamans—or anyone for that matter—walk on hot coals without being burned or pick up embers and place them in their mouths without incident? Simply put, because fire is a field, a frequency the Wixarika call Tatawari'. They call upon this field to offer its powers to cleanse, to help, or to provide support. A few years ago, I had the opportunity to walk on hot coals in a fire ceremony that involved many others. I was apprehensive, so I called upon the spirit of Tatawari', the field of fire, to accompany me and make sure I did not suffer burns. Tatawari' told me to become one with the fire, so I imagined myself as the fire and then walked over the coals without adverse effects.

When we are feeling playful, it is because we have either entered the field of play unconsciously, or because we have deliberately invoked it. Fields are not exclusive. In other words, we may be in the field of play at the same time that we are in the field of gratitude, love, or connectedness. You may choose to go to a concert or festival where thousands of people are invoking the same field all at once, making it much easier for you yourself to access it. On the other hand, if you get a painful text message while you're at the festival, you may disconnect from the field of play, even though others are still enjoying it.

Sometimes, another person opens a field for you. For example, the "hugging saint" Amma is known to open the field of love and tenderness for anyone who comes to her for a hug. A famous comedian may be renowned for her ability to open the field of laughter and catharsis for her audience. A skilled musician may be able to open a whole range of fields, from exuberance to heartbreak to solidarity, depending on the needs of his listeners. If you have ever experienced this, you know what a magical moment it can be when a skilled person opens a field! These are all examples of people accessing the web of life and aligning it with their medicine.

Being resonant with a field is like being on the golden line or the golden path of your life—the highest possibility, where there are no obstacles or difficulties. When you stray off that path, you lose resonance with the fields of clarity, beauty, and effectiveness. The difference is night and day. The key is to get back into resonance with the fields that you want to invoke.

Practice: Invoking Energy Fields

This practice can help you develop your own skill at invoking the energy fields you choose and going into resonance with them. For example, if you are feeling lonely and depressed, you can invoke the fields and frequencies of connectedness and participation. When you keep your mind in accord with these fields, experiences of friendship and connection will begin to flow your way. It's all a matter of intention.

1. Start by paying attention to your emotions throughout the day. Learn to see them not as "your" emotions, but as various fields you are experiencing.

2. Ask yourself if the majority of fields with which you've been resonating have been restrictive and difficult, or expansive, inspiring, uplifting, and encouraging. Over a period of several days, make the same evaluation just to see which fields are typical for you during an average day. Ask yourself if you are satisfied to carry out your life within these fields, or whether you would like to turn your dial to different frequencies.

3. When opening and closing fields, it is best to close down fields you no longer wish to experience first, or they may clash with new fields you are opening. To close fields, identify the

fields you are experiencing and issue a command: "Close the field of discouragement." "Close the field of anxiety." "Close the field of feeling victimized." "Close the field of outrage and anger." "Close the field of hopelessness."

4. Issue this command as if you were the commander of the Starship Enterprise. The crew of the starship consists of all your helping spirits, guides, power animals, spiritual advisors, and angelic helpers. You can let them do the work, but you must be the one who takes responsibility for issuing the command.

5. It is always best to do this with strong intention. Visualizing closing a field symbolically adds to the effectiveness. You can flip a switch or turn a dial or some other motion. If you like, you can end with the words: "Make it so."

6. Now identify the field you want to open. Start by making a clear verbal request. For example, if you're feeling confused, you can simply say: "Clarity, please." If you are faced with a public speaking event, you can say: "Inspiration, stability, and humor, please." When you do, these qualities will arise to support you. If

you are feeling afraid, you can simply say: "I call up the field of courage." It will support you instantly.

7. Remember to visualize the condition the field represents in some way. For example, when you open the field of generosity, see yourself giving resources to someone who needs them. When opening the field of confidence, see yourself speaking confidently to an audience.

8. Remember that the fields you closed are still there. You don't get rid of them when you close them; you simply disconnect from them. Closing a field is like changing channels on the radio or television. The old channel is still there and you can switch back to it. But when you close it, it no longer dominates your awareness. You have refocused.

Opening and closing fields with these specific action steps can help you establish the order and conditions you need for greater effectiveness in manifesting your awareness. Think of this practice like reading a menu in a restaurant, as a container in which to work with your focus and your ability to order your world more effectively.

The Extraordinary
Practice of Gathering
in the Whole Universe

This practice fits in several categories. I have chosen to include it here because it has such a strong energetic component. Although it is one of the more complex practices in this book because it involves coordinating your body movements with your intent, it is well worth trying. It is one of my favorite practices and is extremely powerful.

The practice borrows from several different traditions—for example, Qi Gong, the ancient practice developed by shamanic Taoists in China. Simply put, it is a series of body movements and postures patterned after animal movements and stances that can increase vitality by gathering power and energy, storing it, and making it available for instant and automatic release when needed. It combines muscle memory with contemplation to teach your multidimensional self about wellness, health, power, and the unity of all. Another tradition that contributes to this exercise is Toltec shamanism, which draws on an understanding of where energy and power are stored in the physical body.

Having studied both of these traditions, I have chosen to integrate them to create what has proven to be an exceptionally fruitful practice. In order to learn this technique, you will have to first read about it step by step, and then actually do it with the help of your memory. It's not really all that difficult. What I present here is only a prototype that I encourage you to embellish to fit your own sense of what should be included. Be creative. Begin by following my recommended routine, then experiment on your own. Depending on your routine, it can take as little as ten minutes, or as long as a half hour.

The movements require some limberness, so you may need to do a little stretching beforehand. With more practice, you will become more limber. For now, just do the best you can. Here are a few simple, but important, preparatory steps.

+ Preferably do this before eating and drinking first thing in the morning. You can do it at other times of day, but it may be too energizing just before bed.

- Go to the toilet first and eliminate what you need to so you are not distracted by your plumbing.

- If you can, do this outside, because that can make it more powerful and effective. If weather or climate don't permit, you can do it inside, but it is better to have privacy.

- Wear loose, unrestrictive clothing.

- Always breathe in through your nose and out through your mouth.

- Maintain a healthy balance midway between being totally alert and totally relaxed.

- Create a stretch by pulling your bones up toward the sky and grounding your flesh down to the earth.

- Work with your knees slightly bent but never locked, and keep your feet about shoulder-width apart.

- For women, keep your feet pointed slightly outward; for men, keep your feet pointing straight forward. This helps to accommodate the differences in pelvic structures.

- Distribute your weight in the V-shaped space behind the balls of your feet. Maintain a vertical balance between right and left, and front and back.

- Unless otherwise stated, your movements should always be slow and measured, graceful and refined. There is no hurry.

After a short time, these ideas will become second nature to you and you won't have to think about them.

Posture and Movements

Before we move on to the intention practice below, let's first take a look at the physical posture and movements involved.

1. Begin in the standard Qi Gong starter position, standing erect, preferably facing east or the sunrise. Hang your arms down by your sides in the gunslinger position.

2. Keeping your knees unlocked, slowly lower yourself from the waist, letting your hands and arms drop in front of you. Keep your head completely loose as you bend, so that you are looking back under your butt with your arms and hands scraping against the ground (if you can reach that low). Hold this position for a little while.

3. When you are ready, slowly rise up from the waist, still keeping your knees unlocked. Let your vertebrae stack up one by one as you return to an erect position.

4. As you rise, when your hands are just above your knees, move them out to the sides with your palms facing out. As you continue to rise, turn them to face up as your arms stretch out like a great pair of wings, as if you are about to embrace the sky.

5. Bring your head up last, facing forward.

6. Continue to stretch your arms and hands slowly upward, over your head, then slowly turn your palms down, with the fingers of one hand pointing to the other.

7. As you lower them, slide your hands past each other over your head, with your left hand and arm sliding right behind your right hand and arm, and your right hand and arm sliding left in front of your left. As they cross over your head, let your elbows touch your head over your ears if you can. If you can't, do the best you can to approximate this.

8. Your hands should now be on opposite sides of your head, open like shower heads and moving around as if you are showering all around you—behind, to the sides, and in front.

9. After a few moments, slide your hands apart and, with your fingers facing each other about six to eight inches apart and your palms down, bring them down in front of your face, chin, throat, chest, solar plexus, until they arrive at the Tan Tien, your navel.

10. Hook your thumbs over your navel with the rest of your fingers pointing down, forming a kind of diamond or fig leaf. Hold this position for a time. Then repeat the whole set of movements as many times as you need in order to get them down smoothly. Don't worry. This sounds way more complicated than it actually is.

Practice: Embracing the Whole Universe

Once you have mastered the postures and movements described above, you are ready to begin the actual practice. The important thing is to empty your mind of all thoughts and distractions so that you can reach out to the whole universe and embrace it. This can be challenging, and learning how will slow you way down at first, but that is fine. Take your time.

1. Begin in the position described above, standing erect, preferably facing east or the sunrise, with your arms hanging down by your sides in the gunslinger position.

2. To extent that you are able, empty your mind of all thoughts.

3. Slowly, keeping your knees unlocked, lower yourself from the waist, letting your hands and arms drop in front of you and keeping your head completely loose so that you are looking back under your butt with your arms and hands scraping the ground. Hold that position for a little while, perhaps for several minutes, as you contemplate the thoughts described below. You can imagine all these things in any order, singly, or in any combination you like. Be creative.

4. Imagine you are dropping into the field of Pachamama, the great Earth Mother. The energy of the Earth Mother is enveloping your whole body. You feel incredibly grateful for her gifts. You imagine how powerful she

is, her vitality, her incredible creativity, her phenomenal fertility. All the animals, all the plants, all the minerals, the precious and semi-precious stones. Her fossil records, her layers of sandstone, granite, feldspar, gravel, lava, coal seams, oil, tar, and gases from ancient forests. Her tectonic plates forming mountain ranges, river valleys, plains, hills, badlands, swamps, forested lands, jungles, ice fields, ice caps, frozen lands, hot deserts, temperate climates. Her flowered fields, her coastal regions, her dry and humid regions. Her cool breezes, warm winds, raging tempests, steady rains, hail and sleet, torrential downpours, drizzle, freezing winds, snow, ice storms, avalanches, earthquakes, hurricanes, and tornados. Her oceans, lakes, reservoirs, and lagoons. Her great rivers, creeks, waterfalls, and cascades. Her islands and lava flows, her volcanoes and caverns. Her ancient ruins and modern cities, and all the man-made objects, the human presence. And anything else you can think of that makes up the grand experience of the Earth Mother—her endless patience, her generosity, her love and care for us as she provides for all our needs, asking nothing in return.

5. When you are ready, rise up slowly from the waist, keeping your knees unlocked. Bring your head up last, facing forward. As you rise, when your hands are just above your knees, move them out to the sides with your palms facing out. As you continue to rise, turn them to face up as your arms stretch out like a great pair of wings, as if you are about to embrace the sky.

6. First embrace the moon and all her gifts with great gratitude—her magnetism, her reflected light, her great beauty. Then embrace all the planets in our solar system (you can name them or just intend to embrace them all). Embrace their power, their beauty, their gifts, with great gratitude.

7. Embrace the sun and all its light and dynamism, its life-giving powers. Then embrace the Milky Way, our own galaxy, with all its splendor, its immensity, its light. Do this with great gratitude.

8. Continue to stretch your arms and hands out to the sides and upward over your head as you embrace all the galaxies in the universe, with all

their suns, planets, moons, gas clouds, asteroids, comets, black holes, black and white dwarves, supernovas, and radio waves. Embrace all intelligent life forms. Embrace hydrogen, nitrogen, oxygen, and all chemistries. Embrace everything known and unknown that may be out there.

9. As your arms reach a position over your head, embrace Spirit, God, everything and nothing, the supreme intelligence of the universe. Embrace love, gratitude, and awe, all time, all space, all possibilities, all creativity, and fertility. Then gather everything you have named and even everything you have not named into one tiny unit over your head.

10. As you lower your hands, slide them by each other, left hand and arm behind, right hand and arm in front. As you cross them over your head, let your elbows touch your head over your ears if you can. If you can't, just do the best you can to approximate this.

11. With your hands now on opposite sides of your head, open them like shower heads and move them around as if you are showering all around you—behind, to the sides, and in front.

What you are showering around yourself is everything you have gathered on the way up.

12. After a few moments, slide your hands apart and, with your fingers facing each other about six to eight inches apart and your palms down, bring them down in front of your face, continuing to pour the entire universe into your crown and Third Eye, opening up your own supreme intelligence, knowing, perception, clarity, and understanding.

13. Bring your hands down past your chin and throat, opening up all your strength and power, filling you with self-esteem and self-expression, and pushing out all self-deprecation, judgments, and repression.

14. Bring your hands down in front of your chest, filling you with all the love, compassion, gratitude, forgiveness, generosity, and kindness of the universe. Push out all grief, sadness, depression, and anger.

15. Bring your hands down to your solar plexus, filling you with health and well-being, and pushing out all illness and imbalances. Then

bring them down in front of your navel, filling you with the highest possibilities of this lifetime and good new paths to walk. Wash away all dead ends, frustrations, and distractions.

17. Hook your thumbs over your navel and point the rest of your fingers down, forming a kind of diamond or fig leaf. Hold this position for a time. Then repeat the whole set of movements a second or, ideally, even a third time.

Do this once a day, every day for a month. If you like, you can continue for much longer. You will not regret it.

PART THREE

Relational Practices

In Native American communities, it is customary to use the phrase "all my relations" at the end of a prayer, acknowledging not only our ancestors and human relatives, but the plants and animals who make up our wider community. In Buddhism, meditators dedicate their practice to "the benefit of all beings." Christians pray for God to forgive both their own trespasses and those who have trespassed against them. It's clear that all these traditions teach that remembering and tending to our relationships is key to spiritual progress.

The practices in this section are all about affirming and upholding our relationships with humans, with animals, and with life itself. When we realize that we exist in a state of divine relationship with all beings, it becomes easier to love, to forgive, to share, and to be kind and show compassion.

The Extraordinary Practice
of Seeing Through
the Eyes of Spirit

In this world, we are conditioned from a young age by social norms, by family, by subcultures, and by national pride to evaluate and judge others according to many factors—the color of their skin, their gender, their heritage, their language, their financial status, their beliefs and religious preferences, their sexual preferences, and many other things. We are subtly trained to sort people into acceptable and unacceptable groups, often with dire consequences for those we choose to reject. We may even consider these evaluations to be normal and natural. Yet they are anything but.

In the shamanic understanding, the web of life includes everything and everyone without exception. All humans are considered to be expressions of Spirit. A rejection of self or a rejection of anyone else is therefore a rejection of Spirit itself. Another way of saying this is that we cannot reject any aspect of the web of life without rejecting ourselves. Most people today do not have shamanic training and, unfortunately, most religions have forgotten this most fundamental principle. In fact, many officially call for the rejection of others outside their religion.

The habit of judging others and rejecting them is truthfully a rejection of the one Spirit that created everything—and that includes ourselves. The results of this are truly disastrous to our well-being and happiness, because when you deny good will toward others, you automatically bring immediate rejection back on yourself. This means that if you refuse to shine your light on others, they cannot shine that light back on you, just as you cannot shine sunlight on others if the sun does not shine on you. This may seem quite obvious to some, but it is not yet understood by the majority.

There is a very simple solution to this problem. We simply have to learn to see through the eyes of Spirit. We have to learn to see others the way Spirit sees them. But how do we know how Spirit sees us? How do you see your newborn child? How do you see flowers, plants, trees, birds flying? How do you see fish swimming, the breeze blowing ripples on the surface of a pond, a cloud forming in the sky? If you are a healthy human being, you see these things with delight and with joy. And that is how Spirit sees them and us, as its most precious children. That is the way Spirit sees all of us.

Practice: Aligning with the Web of Life

This simple practice can help you move out of an attitude of judgment and exclusion into alignment with the web of life. It is well worth doing.

1. Begin by seeing people as brand new, without any preconceived notions other than that they are as they are—perfect versions of themselves. See how they are alive; know they are alive. See how they are fully aware of themselves as human, just as you are aware that you are alive every moment of your day. Do this with family, friends, colleagues, and neighbors.

2. Practice seeing people without thinking or judging, without evaluating, just as you would do as you watch a hummingbird fly. The hummingbird just is. So is everything else.

3. If you want to challenge yourself, practice watching people in a public place, including those you may have had trouble accepting in the past. Look past your own racial, gender, status, and age stereotypes.

4. Silently say any of these phrases as you watch total strangers in a public place: "I see you as Spirit sees you—full of majesty and beauty, and deserving of love." "I see you as filled with light." "I know who you are—an expression of Spirit." "I know what you are, fully human for now." "I know your mission—to see everything as Spirit."

5. Up the ante whenever you think you are ready to go one step further. Move beyond the people you are watching and think of politicians, historical figures, and others about whom you have made judgments. Consider those who belong to religions of which you may disapprove, or political parties with which you disagree. In fact, try to see everyone as Spirit sees them.

6. Remind yourself that at some moments of your life you too have behaved badly. You too have been greedy, aggressive, or self-serving. You too have operated out of fear or delusion.

7. Once you have identified a thread of similarity between yourself and those you dislike or the strangers you have been observing, allow yourself to see that, just like you, they may

be immature and acting from ego, according to their current beliefs about what is best for them. They too want to survive, and this is the only way they think they can.

8. Remind yourself that we are all on an evolutionary path. Just like you, everyone is on their way to becoming an enlightened being and may even one day become a great spiritual teacher — perhaps your spiritual guide in another time and place.

9. Pray for the liberation and ultimate happiness of the people you observe. Allow yourself to see them in their right to be alive and in their magnificence as living beings.

No one said this would be an easy practice, but it is simple. It just takes — well, practice. Do this often for very short periods of time and see what happens.

Whether you work with this practice on occasion or even every day, you will feel happier. You will also find that you no longer judge yourself or reject yourself as much, just as you have ceased judging and rejecting others.

The Extraordinary Practice
of Blessing Everyone

I grew up with a Mexican Catholic mother and grand-
mother. Both of them regularly blessed my brother and
me by making the sign of the cross and saying: "Dios te
bendiga, mi hito," which means "God bless you, son."
When I went to church, the priests and bishop blessed
the congregation with Latin prayers, or by sprinkling
holy water, or by walking down the aisle swinging a
censer of fragrant incense. It seemed to me that blessing
others was a beautiful and mysterious act, which could
either be intensely solemn or as warm and familiar as
coming home.

As an adult, my wife and I began to study with a
Wixarika *maracame*, or shaman, who blessed us by dip-
ping a flower in water and shaking the water all over
us and our offerings. These blessings often took place
in the freezing Sonoran Desert in central Mexico, first
thing in the morning after an all-night peyote ceremony.

The water was icy, but somehow it felt delicious. And this is when I learned that you don't have to be a priest, or a minister, or a bishop to bless others. Spirit blesses others through us when we have sincere intentions and self-authorization. Later, when I spent time with the Qero people in the Andes, I learned about their concept of an advanced shaman being a "walking blessing." They taught me that we should all aspire to bless everyone, everywhere, all the time.

The word "bless" comes from the Old English *bletsian*, which means "to consecrate (with blood)." In ancient times, it was thought that sprinkling a little blood on something in the spirit of sacrifice would make that thing holy. Nowadays, we are more likely to associate this word with holy water, with words spoken by a priest or spiritual teacher, or as related to phrases like "count your blessings." As we saw in the last practice, the actual act of blessing others is that we see them as they truly are—an expression of Spirit. The water we may sprinkle on them represents the aliveness and beingness that Spirit has bestowed upon them. Thus a blessing is a reminder of what is true.

Although many of us feel very grateful for blessings we have received, it rarely occurs to us that we, too, are capable of blessing others. But blessing is not an act reserved for ordained priests or respected gurus; it is an act of love available to all of us, all the time. When we bless others, we share our own light and remind them of their own inherent goodness and worth.

Blessing others can take many forms. Often, we bless others with our speech—by paying them a compliment, wishing them well, comforting and encouraging them, or affirming that we see, love, and value them. Everybody needs their spirits lifted from time to time, and a few sincere and loving words can sometimes be exactly the blessing we need to carry on. We also bless others by performing random acts of kindness—being generous, patient, and forgiving, or sharing our joyful energy. Knowing that you have received tremendous blessings from life, it becomes easy to bless others in turn.

The following practice shows you a third way to bless others—by silently wishing them well. Although it is wonderful to bless others with your words and actions, there are times when it isn't possible or practical to have an interaction with those you want to bless. In cases like this, you can carry out the act of blessing on a completely internal basis. You may even begin to realize how many people there are out there in the world who have silently been blessing you!

Practice: Sending Silent Blessings

In this practice, you go to a place where many people are gathered, such as a mall or a sidewalk café on a busy street, and find a place to sit. When you are comfortably settled, follow these simple steps.

1. Focus your awareness and inwardly speak a positive affirmation—for instance: "All is divine, as am I." This is the best place to begin when you are blessing—with an expression of Spirit.

2. As you watch people going by, silently wish them love, happiness, and good health. Bless them and extend total benevolence to them, no matter whether they are young or old, rich or poor. See them as they are—an expression of Spirit.

3. If you like, you can silently speak a wish for each person you bless. For example: "May you be happy." "May you be healthy." "May you be free from all suffering."

4. Imagine that your blessing has been received, and that the people in question are feeling a tiny bit lighter for reasons they don't quite understand. This is not a wish, but a fact.

5. As you bless others, notice yourself becoming happier and more blessed in turn.

Remember, those you bless bless you back in multiple ways. To stretch the point a wee bit further, *whatever* you bless blesses you back in myriad ways. If you want your life to be a blessing, start blessing.

The Extraordinary
Practice of Prayer

When I was a child in Catholic school, praying was something my classmates and I had to do every day, in the same way we mumbled the Pledge of Allegiance. As part of confession, the priest even assigned prayer as a kind of punishment—twenty Hail Marys for lying, ten Our Fathers for swearing, and so on. I rattled off those prayers one after another, eager to get them over with. For the longest time, I had no idea that prayer could be sincere, moving, or emotional—that it could bring about a catharsis or other important changes in my life.

It was only when I began to study with my Wix-arika teacher that I learned a different kind of prayer—a prayer that was deep, wholehearted, and pulsing with life. This man had a more vital connection with Spirit than anyone I had ever met. He taught me that *el Dios*, as he called God, answered any question we asked of him— we just had to learn how to speak to him with a completely open heart. He also taught me the importance of speaking to God frequently and intimately—not just rattling off prayers before bed, but conversing with God as a friend and confidante throughout the day. When he talked about God, he often cried. To him, God was not a concept, but an immediate presence. He taught me to experience God in the same way.

Ever since my apprenticeship with this teacher, I have come to love and cherish the act of prayer. My prayers are no longer dry and hurried, but deeply personal and heartfelt. When I pray the way he taught me, the results are unmistakable. I never fail to receive the strength, guidance, love, or forgiveness I ask for. Although my prayers these days most often take the form of spontaneous dialogues with Spirit, I also have a deep appreciation for more structured prayers like the Serenity Prayer and the powerful prayer I have included in the following practice. Structured prayers are wonderful when you're lost for words or when you want to tap into a powerful collective energy, merging your own prayers with those of a group or with the prayers of millions of others who are using the same words.

Practice: Praying to the Great Spirit

In this practice, I share a prayer that was given to me many years ago by a Sikh woman who was treating me with deep-tissue body work. You can use it, as I have, as a starting point for developing your own practice. It consists of a series of statements invoking love, good health, and other positive states of being. When you make this prayer with sincerity and an open heart, you will find that these positive states come to you easily. You can use it for yourself or for others you wish to benefit.

Prepare by calming your breathing and quieting your mind. Then say the following prayer from the heart. As you move through these phrases, let your speech fall into a rhythm, creating a slightly altered state. Allow your mind to quiet down, and let yourself be transported by the timeless sense of the words.

> *Hail, Hail, Hail Honored Great Spirit*
> *Heal me; bless me with health, wealth,*
> *prosperity, intuition, compassion, light,*
> *laughter, peace.*
>
> *Honored Great Spirit*
> *Heal me; bless me with health, wealth,*
> *prosperity, intuition, compassion, light,*
> *laughter, peace.*
> *Honored Great Spirit*
> *Heal me; bless me with health in my mind,*
> *body, and spirit, that it may glow.*

Bless me with wealth that it may grow.
Bless me with prosperity, intuition,
compassion that it may flow.
Bless me with light and laughter that it may
show and give me peace that I may know
grace, humility, and serenity.

Inspire me with loving, beautiful
environments in my home and in my
work; may these places nurture me,
rejuvenate me, relax me, and energize me,
and inspire me with loving, supportive relationships.

Surround me always with people of
consciousness and caliber, people who
will elevate me and support me in my
higher consciousness so that I in turn may
have compassion for others.

All blessings, all blessings, all blessings, light,
love, support to me and my loved ones
from the past, through my present to my future.

As you pray, connect to the energy of all the other living beings all over the world who are praying for the same things you are. Feel your prayers joining with theirs—a beautiful river of prayer flowing toward the source of all life. Become aware of the qualities you are praying for manifesting in your mind, your body, and your heart.

When you feel complete, say a few words of gratitude to Spirit, and make any physical gesture (like bowing or joining your palms together) that feels significant to you.

The Extraordinary Practice of Speaking with Your Higher Self

I once had to fly to another city to do some consultation work. My client's agent sent me a copy of the flight schedule, which revealed that I'd been assigned a middle seat in the very back of the plane. I sighed, a little disappointed, but didn't think much of it. After all, it was only a three-hour flight.

On the day of the flight, I had my usual conversation with my higher self—the part of me that is wise, loving, and expansive, and that seems to "know" things that can't always be explained. I then drove myself to the airport in a snowstorm, hoping the flight would not be canceled. Upon getting to the airport, I discovered that the flight was on time. When I got to my gate, I looked at my boarding pass and saw that I was in group one for boarding, which I attributed to being a gold member. I had some time to wait before the flight left, so I sat and had another little conversation with my higher self.

"I'd really like to get a window seat," I told my higher self, "so that I can lean my head against the side of the plane and get a little sleep. I had to get up at 2:30 this morning to catch this flight, and I'd hate to be tired for my consultation session later today."

I heard my higher self say: "Just relax and don't worry about it. Spend your time here blessing all the people boarding this flight." I followed these instructions and had a very good time doing just that instead of reading the news on my smartphone. I then boarded the plane fully prepared for the usual sardine experience in the cramped quarters of economy class.

When I got on the plane, however, I finally looked at my seat number and could barely believe my eyes. I had an aisle seat in business class! But it didn't end there. The man sitting in the window seat behind me tapped me on the shoulder and asked me if I would like to change seats with him because he wanted to sit next to his wife, who was now sitting next to me. I grinned broadly and agreed. I'm sure he had no idea what I was grinning about.

It seemed to me that, by listening to my higher self and following its advice to relax and let go of my worries, I had somehow manifested exactly what I wanted. But even if I hadn't gotten that business-class seat, I still would have won, because speaking to my higher self helped me spend my time in a positive way, instead of sitting by the gate preoccupied with anxiety about not being able to sleep on the plane.

Talking to your higher self may not always get you a better seat on an airplane, but it will make you happier, kinder, and more at peace. By tuning in to the part of you that is loving, patient, and wise, you set yourself up for success in every domain of life, whether that be your career, your relationships, or your spiritual life.

Big Self, Small Self

Most of us have two modes from which we operate—our lower self, which is often frightened, selfish, defensive, and concerned with immediate pleasures and pains, and our higher self, which is wise, expansive, and loving. While your lower self—your small self—may be very reactive to life's ups and downs, your higher self—your big self—knows that this physical life is nothing but a very realistic dream. Because your big self operates from beyond the dream, the dream does not frighten it in the least. It knows that this life is just a cartoon created to teach and provide experiences.

Many of us flail around in life, forgetting that it is all a dream. We operate from our small selves, forgetting that our big selves are always available to guide and support us. Meanwhile, this big self is always watching us, like a parent at a playground—refraining from intervening unless we ask it for help. In time, clever and curious children will figure out that their parents can be valuable resources for learning. They may begin to say: "Dad, Mom, could you help me put this puzzle together?" Or "Will you help me put this new bike together and teach me to ride it?" Children want to learn and grow, so they seek out their parents' wisdom.

Likewise, we all have higher selves to whom we can turn for help and advice—and if we learn to listen, we soon discover that they always answer us. Speaking to your higher self is a little bit like praying. You may ask it for guidance, encouragement, or love. The stronger a relationship you forge with it, the more confident and unperturbed you will be as you go about your daily life, knowing that a source of infinite wisdom has your back at all times.

Practice: Conversing with Your Higher Self

Try having a conversation with your higher self every day for thirty days in a row. That conversation might go something like this:

> *Higher Self, I am so glad you are with me. I haven't spoken with you like this in a long while, but I want a strong relationship with you. I could use some help here with my life. I need a good guide that I can trust*

completely. I am prepared to listen to you and follow your advice and guidance. Give me many signs and signals about the right course of action for me. Make it obvious. I don't expect you to do everything for me. I realize this is my dream and I am responsible for it. Just help me to know what the truth is.

Remind me often that I am a sacred being, divine in nature, way more capable than I think I am. Help me to know that I am never alone, that you are always with me, my very best friend. Help me not to judge myself harshly. Help me not to punish myself. Help me to look around and see others, not as they appear, but for who they actually are—other aspects of myself. Help me not to judge them. Keep me from attacking others and seeing them in terms of their flaws. Help me to be compassionate, kind, and generous in all my dealings with myself and others.

I am ready to transform my life. I am ready to release my old familiar ways and to embrace the unknown. I am free of all limitations, all confinement, all lies, all fears, and all false programs. Thank you for listening to me. I love you. I know you love me.

Next, spend a few moments in silence just listening and noticing how you feel. Perhaps you will sense nothing. Perhaps you will feel a presence. Perhaps you will hear some thoughts in your head that you experience as very serene, inducing a profound state of calm, emptiness, or tranquility. You may feel jubilation, joy, or inspiration. You may feel a deep sense of relief, release, or freedom. Whatever you experience, don't judge it. Just notice it, and know that your higher self is there.

If you do not believe you have a higher or core self, that is okay. But consider that most creatures in nature do have a type of core or higher self. The higher self of animals is the archetype of their species—the ultimate hawk-ness of many types of hawks; the spirit of spider for all types of spiders; the archetypal canine at the core of all types of dogs, from Great Danes to chihuahuas. All trees have a core, and a seed as their source. Volcanoes have an inner core. Each flower reveals its higher self, its archetypal species. While human beings have a body that functions largely in a stimulus-response mode, what unites all humans is our ultimate awareness that we are alive and present, our awareness of being aware. This is the expression of the higher self in humans, our archetypal design.

All the great teachers in all spiritual traditions teach that connecting to the higher self is the key to evolution, to happiness, and to freedom. You can deny that or accept it. But if you do accept it, your life is going to be a lot easier—like hopping onto a motorcycle after pushing along on a skateboard. To put it simply, your higher self is your greatest ally for all endeavors, and it responds without fail when you ask it to.

The Extraordinary Practice
of Aligning with Spirit

The lower self is not capable of truly knowing who or what it is. It bumbles along in life in a frightened state, doing the best it can to carve a path through the jungle of life according to its own definition of success by striving to stave off misfortune. The definition of success it holds is important, because this has to do with how it manifests its experience of the world. Perhaps it believes that life is competitive and it needs to struggle to overcome all opponents in order to achieve success. Perhaps it believes that being in control of every detail in life is the path to conquering the world. This may mean trying to control everyone else as well. Perhaps it believes that, although it needs love, love makes it vulnerable to manipulation and therefore is a luxury it cannot afford. This is not the fault of the lower self, however, because it truly believes it is alone in the world and separate from everything else.

All humans have a lower self that behaves something like this and has its own unique and creative signature. What this self does *not* know is that it is doomed to failure, because it has no real power to accomplish its mission. That is not its fault, either; it is just what is so. A six-year-old is not capable of performing the tasks that a forty-year-old can. No blame there. This is simply what is obvious.

In shamanic terms, we each have our own medicine path, but we are often unaware of this because our families, our subculture, our religion, and our conditioning may have other plans for us. The important thing is to discover what our own medicine path is before it is too late to act on it.

The power to accomplish our life task, to walk our medicine path, can only come from what Native Americans call the spirit world, and this requires acknowledging that nothing can be accomplished without aligning to that great force. This means surrendering our lower selves' plans and desires to a higher mission, one that is in alignment with Spirit, one that will lead to satisfaction and fulfillment instead of some short-term tenuous success. The lower self doesn't want anything to do with surrendering. Yet surrender it must, and if that means being brought to its knees, then so be it. But it's not really necessary to suffer a serious blow to make the shift. We can do it out of choice and suffer very little for it—except for perhaps a jolt to our expectations and a brief bump to our pride.

Many think making this shift means becoming a servant of God and giving up everything pleasurable in life—wearing hair shirts, or shaving their heads, or making similar sacrifices. Although there is nothing inherently wrong with these behaviors, they are quite unnecessary and may even be a hidden source of piousness and pride. Spirit—the Creator, God—is not looking for servants or slaves, nor does it want us to surrender our will. That is not the relationship it wants to have with us. Spirit *is* us and wants us to be fulfilled and satisfied. It wants us to be co-partners, revenue-sharing partners, if you will. It wants its will and ours to be in alignment, to be co-resonant, to be harmonious. Spirit doesn't ask that we surrender and become slaves, because there is no power in that. That is a hierarchical relationship in which it has no interest. Spirit wants us to step up, to demonstrate maturity and master skillful means. How could we do that if we didn't have our own will and make our own choices—and mistakes?

Practice: Walking Your Medicine Path

This extraordinarily simple practice takes almost no time. But it can help you shift your entire life plan to align with your own medicine path. It can take the form of a simple prayer or statement of fact. It is almost like writing up a simple contract or declaration that you remind yourself of daily in creative new ways.

1. Take a brief moment to become aware of your will, the part of you that has desires and wishes and the motivation to fulfill them through whatever means you have. Sense the part of your body that carries your will. For many, it is the right leg, the thighs and hamstrings; for some, it is the arms and hands or the shoulders; for others, it is the jaw with a firm determination in the eyes. Wherever it is, feel its presence.

2. Get in touch with what your will desires at this time. Where are you headed and for what reasons? Is that what you really want as an overall goal? Or is it temporary and local? Go for the big picture.

3. Connect with your higher self—your core self that is aligned at all times with Spirit. You may feel this presence above you or behind you, or deep in your heart. When the great spiritual traditions of the world say that this core self resides in the heart, they are not referring to our physical hearts or to a physical location.

They are referring to a dimension that we could simply call the "heart of all hearts."

4. Imagine that you could go to this heart of all hearts and simply rest there. Now reach out to Spirit, saying something like this:

Hi Spirit, I am discovering that you are all around me and I am inside you and you are inside me. I recognize that this is how interwoven we are. So what I call my life is actually your life too and your life is mine. Since you created me and my life, it is actually yours and I want you to have it. I give it to you so that you can express yourself through me in the best ways possible.

At this time, I choose to align my will to yours, Spirit. I know that your will and your plans for me are for my highest well-being and satisfaction and I couldn't do better with my own plans for myself. Lift me up to vibrate harmoniously with your grand plan for me. I accept this partnership with pleasure and anticipation that this sharing of our wills will be beyond my wildest expectations. I freely accept the unknown; I accept the challenge. I accept with all my heart, with all my strength, with my whole mind,

*without reservation. Teach me. Show me the
way to my medicine path. Make it so obvious
and clear that I can't possibly miss it. Help me
to drop any expectations that lead me in a direction that is not fulfilling. Thank you, Spirit, for
everything. May it be so.*

You may even choose to write this statement up as a
document and place it where you can read it every day.

The Extraordinary Practice
of Asking for Help

Anytime, anywhere, under any circumstances, help is available for anything you need. In fact, there is never a time or place or situation in which you can't ask for help, because this is entirely a personal, private concern that can take place completely silently in your mind. From a shamanic perspective, you are absolutely free to request assistance or guidance at all times and are unreservedly encouraged to do so in whatever manner you choose—by singing, chanting, praying, speaking out loud, commanding, directing, or silently requesting it sincerely and with strong intent. You can ask for help for yourself, for your family, for friends, for situations and events, for conditions, and for the world at large without limitation. And the best part is that help is always free, except for its costs to your former behaviors or beliefs.

The good news is that almost everyone learns to ask for help when they meet with difficulties and challenges on their path through life. Most often, this practice begins when we are children and ask adults and older siblings for help standing up, or reaching what is high up, or tying our shoes, or many other little things we cannot do yet. This practice is revived when we grow old and require physical help all over again. Between these stages, we learn to do things for ourselves and enjoy the challenges life presents to us.

Nevertheless, life will always present us with situations that may force us to ask for help, whether it is to do our taxes, resolve a health problem, recover from an accident, deal with a troubled relative, raise our children, overcome PTSD, or face an addiction. Unfortunately, some of us become too proud to ask for help or simply forget to ask, thinking that we have to solve all problems all by ourselves. Of course, life can be so much harder when we don't ask for help, especially when we are overwhelmed or at a dead end.

A huge part of shamanic practice is based on regularly asking for help—from allies, guides, ancestors, saints, elementals, local spirits, deities, angelic beings, and, of course, Spirit itself. In fact, trained shamans wouldn't think of going it alone, especially when it comes to healing, conducting ceremonies, or doing their special work. Shamans cultivate special relationships with animal totems and elementals, *ayudantes* (helpers), and *poderios* (powerful allies) throughout their lives, talking and singing to them, giving them offerings, and mentally asking them for their guidance and assistance.

At the end of the day, it doesn't matter at all whom you ask for help, as long as you have a belief in their power to help you. Catholics pray to Jesus, the Holy Spirit, the saints, and Mother Mary for help. Muslims pray to Allah; Hindus pray to Brahma, Vishnu, Shiva, Sarasvati, Lakshmi, Kali, and a whole pantheon of gods and goddesses. Native Americans pray to the Great Spirit, and this is the same all over the world in various traditions. The main thing to understand is that help is everywhere you turn, as summarized by the prayer: "Wherever we are, God is!"

Practice: Asking . . . and Listening

Actually requesting help is really quite simple. First, identify what you need help with. Then phrase your request as a question. Or you can make it more of a statement or even a command, if you are already in the habit of working with certain helpers. For example, if you need help deciding where to vacation, you can ask the question: "Should I travel to Cancún for my vacation, or would Guatemala be best?" Or you can phrase it as a request: "Please help me determine where it would be best for me to vacation this year." You can even be more direct: "I need some help determining where to go on vacation this year. Give me a clear message as soon as possible."

There are a couple of important considerations, however. It is never a good idea to presume anything or make assumptions about what the answer may be. So be sure to phrase your request carefully. For example, instead of assuming you know the best course of action and asking for that, it is better to ask for the best possible outcome in this situation. Although you may be attached to what you consider the best outcome, in the long run that may not be the best outcome, or even good for you at all. So instead of stating that you want help making a new love interest work out, try saying: "I want help clarifying what this new relationship should be." Or "Please support the best possibility for this new relationship."

A major part of this practice is paying attention to the responses you get to your request for help. These may come instantly or over a period of time. Of course, the response may be a direct change in your experience—like suddenly getting well from an illness or a dramatic recovery from a wound or an accident. But some responses may come in various other ways. Many receive responses in their dreams or suddenly, out of the blue, in a creative thought or clear insight. These types of responses often come in the form of symbols or images that require some interpretation or decoding. For example, upon requesting help in a business endeavor, you may have a dream or receive an image that shows you flying in a plane or perhaps walking down a street in Tokyo. This may lead you to understand that travel may be a necessary aspect of your business deal. In other words, there may be a creative aspect to your understanding of the response.

You can certainly simplify the whole process by asking clear questions of your guides or allies. If you are ill, for example, you can ask: "What is the lesson?" Or "What can I learn from this situation?" Or "What is the message in this experience?" Once you get clarity on the lesson, you can heal or set the situation straight much more quickly, because there is no longer any need for it.

And always remember to thank your helpers for their assistance and help. While they do not require it and certainly never ask you to be grateful, they do appreciate your respect and sincerity. Remember that gratitude is more helpful for you than for them.

Try not to be frivolous with your requests. In other words, don't be lazy. There are many choices and decisions you can make for yourself. You don't need help deciding whether to have chocolate or vanilla ice cream for dessert, or what kind of haircut to get. Don't waste your guides' valuable help with questions like these. Be responsible and ask for assistance when you genuinely need it. Then your guides will take you seriously every time.

And most important, you need to develop the habit of *listening* to the advice you get. If you ask for help, you will definitely get it in some way. But you need to consider what that guidance actually means. I have found my guides and helpers to be highly accurate. In fact, I have never known them to be wrong, and this has actually saved my life on a couple of occasions. Defy them or ignore them at your own peril.

The Extraordinary Practice of Visiting Your Future Self

What if you could make contact with your future self—the self who knows all the consequences of the decisions you're making right now, and the outcomes of situations that currently seem so precarious and uncertain? The one who has lived through all of the beginnings and endings, joys and sorrows, victories and losses of your life—everything that has made up your time here on earth. The one who has a broad perspective on the issues that feel so all-consuming to you right now.

Although many of us like to fantasize about future events—a long-awaited vacation, the birth of a child, or a reunion with a friend or lover—it's relatively rare for us to contemplate our own elderhood, especially if that time is still years or decades away. We put a lot of thought into the near future, while giving the distant future a lot less attention. Yet in North America, 65 percent of people will live past age eighty, while 35 percent will live into their nineties. In other words, the vast majority of us will indeed grow old.

Study after study has shown that those who feel a strong sense of connection to their future selves make better decisions in the present day—exercising, saving money, and even acting more ethically. Just as meditating on death can make you more grateful for life, contemplating old age can inspire you to take better care of your body, invest in your relationships, and live a life that you will be proud of later. Just visualizing your own face and body at ninety years old or writing a letter to your elderly self can lead to dramatic shifts in behavior. Just ask the study participants who started exercising once a week and continued to exercise for at least six months, after doing the following practice just once!

Practice: Connecting with the Future You

This practice gives you the opportunity to strengthen the connection between your current self and your future self through visualization. If you do it on a regular basis, you'll find that it clarifies your values and shows you what you really care about. And this can help you become the person you want to be.

1. Sit in a comfortable position and take a moment to clear your mind. Close your eyes and ask for a helping spirit, a guide, an angel, or

an ally to lead you on this short journey to visit your wise and more experienced future self—a self who has gained perspective and a clear sense of identity, and who has discovered their own medicine and is using it well.

2. When you feel ready, with the assistance of your ally, visualize yourself at a particular time in your future—six months from now, five or ten years in the future, or even when you are very old, perhaps at the end of your life. Picture yourself as you will look at whatever time you choose.

3. Notice how you will look and feel as that person. Let yourself feel a connection with this future version of yourself. Send love forward in time to your future self and feel that love being sent back to you. If you like, you can make a silent request for guidance.

4. Now imagine facing this future self and looking closely into their eyes. Imagine that you actually become part of them and look out through their eyes at your present-day self, complete with all your current dilemmas and challenges. How does your future self feel to you? More stable? Neutral? Powerful? Compassionate and kind? Wise?

5. What does this older version of yourself want to tell you that might be helpful for your current situation?

6. What does this future self want your present-day self to know? Would they tell you not to worry so much about the matters that preoccupy your thoughts? Would they encourage you to take that risk you've been too timid to attempt? Would they gently remind you to take better care of yourself? Invest more in your relationships? Live your life with more integrity and authenticity?

7. When this exchange is complete, imagine jumping back into your present-day self and feeling that this future self is not a separate person, but is *you*. Bless this future version of yourself and see them as an expression of God who is on their authentic medicine path.

Visit your future self on a regular basis. Keep this person in mind as you make small and large life decisions, in the same way you would consider the needs of a partner or child. Remember that you can visit your future self at different ages, and in different time frames, whenever it is convenient.

The Extraordinary Practice of Looking Beyond Your Life

The French philosopher Pierre Teilhard de Chardin famously wrote: "We are not human beings having a spiritual experience, we are spiritual beings having a human experience." His words have become something of an anthem among spiritual seekers, and I believe they are completely accurate. Teilhard de Chardin suggests that we are multidimensional beings—in other words, beings who transcend their ordinary bodies and personalities, beings who encompass past lives, possible futures, the subconscious, and the higher self. If you've ever experienced synchronicity, feelings of déja vu, or strong unexplained intuitions, then you know the mysterious thrill of feeling two dimensions of yourself briefly intersecting. And if you work with spiritual practices on a regular basis, you may find that these experiences occur with greater and greater frequency.

In the modern world, we are taught that the material world is all that exists, and that the bodies and personalities we have in this lifetime are all that we are. We lose sight of the fact that "the individual" is a social construct—an idea, not a biological fact. For example, our bodies are home to a plenitude of nonhuman organisms—millions of tiny creatures that both are and are not "us." We share our DNA with many plants and animals. And thanks to something known as "mirror neurons"—neurons that mirror the behavior of others as though we ourselves were acting—we can't even claim that our emotions are our own. We feel the emotions of the people around us, whether we like it or not, and project our own emotions onto others in turn.

Shamanic cultures emphasize this multidimensional, interdependent aspect of life. By connecting with the spirits of plants, animals, and natural features like rocks and lakes, shamans break down the illusion of a strict separation between the human and nonhuman worlds. By journeying to past and future lives, they dissolve the illusion of linear, one-directional time. And by concerning themselves with the well-being of all creatures—not just that very special creature we call "myself"—shamans truly become walking blessings, spreading love and healing wherever they go.

Practice: Discovering Your Infinite Self

In the previous practice, you visualized your future self. In this practice, you will do just the opposite—visualize a progressively younger version of yourself, until you come face-to-face with your own existence before you were born. "Show me your original face before you were born," a Zen koan enjoins. In a similar way, this practice encourages you to break down the illusion of a separate self and puts you in touch with the infinite potential of the universe.

1. Sit in a comfortable position and take a moment to clear your mind.

2. Start to visualize yourself growing younger and younger, moving backward through your life as if you were slowly rewinding a tape.

3. See yourself as you were five years ago, ten years ago. See yourself as an adolescent, then as a child, then as a baby. As you do this, imagine that you are releasing the energy of all the events that you believe you experienced in the narrative of your life. Release maladies, physical conditions stemming from accidents and illnesses, aging problems, disappointments, and failures. Release, release, release. Your so-called official history is only a narrative, an idea of yourself. But the person you have been encompasses many other possibilities and ideas.

4. As you move backward through the years, send love to all these previous versions of yourself, and feel them sending love to the present-day you.

5. When you reach the infant version of yourself, don't stop! Visualize yourself as a fetus, then as a tiny bundle of cells, then as whatever your being was before those cells formed. What were you before you were born? Energy? Spirit? Light? A guide for others? A different human in a different time?

6. Whatever the answer, send love to this place, and feel it sending love back to you in the present day. After all, it's all happening now.

The Extraordinary Practice
of Shapeshifting into
Animal Consciousness

At every moment of every day, we are surrounded by other forms of consciousness—not only the consciousness of the people around us, but of every bird, squirrel, spider, insect, and other creature in our environment. As children, many of us played at being animals. We were instinctively drawn to hop like frogs, bark like dogs, and climb like monkeys. Some of us were so fascinated by other life forms that we spent hours peering at tadpoles in a pond, worms in the grass, or chipmunks scurrying up and down trees. As children, it seemed natural to be attuned to the presence of other life forms, and in constant spontaneous communication with other creatures.

In modern Western society, however, this tendency is all too often bred out of us by the educational system, which teaches us to pay attention to letters and numbers instead of living things. We learn to memorize facts about trees and animals instead of entering into relationship with them. As we grow older, we give up the "childish" game of "trying on" the consciousness of other animals, and become more and more boxed in by our human way of seeing, sensing, and perceiving. By the time we are adults, many of us have more or less forgotten all about the insects, fish, and mammals that so fascinated us as children. We live out our days within the confines of a strictly human bubble, having strictly human experiences.

In shamanic traditions, this state of isolation is seen as a very sad, if not downright insane, way to live. For many shamanic peoples, putting oneself in the consciousness of a bird, a deer, or another animal is a way of gaining wisdom and perspective that is hard to access from a human point of view. All over the world, shamans practice the art of shapeshifting—looking at the world through the eyes of a spider, or flying with the wings of a hawk, or moving with the grace of a deer. Shapeshifting helps them forge a closer relationship with the medicine of other creatures.

Experiencing the world through the body of a deer can put you in touch with the deer's way of being; putting yourself in the consciousness of a bear can give you the experience of strength and power and maternal protectiveness. In shamanism, this is not considered just an imaginative exercise, but an actuality. Shamans *become* the animal. And with much practice, they may appear to others as that animal when they wish to.

Practice: "Trying On" Other Forms of Consciousness

This practice allows you to recapture the joy, the wonder, and the wisdom of "trying on" the consciousness of the animals in your environment, and to reclaim your innate capacity for relationship with other forms of life. I like to connect with the consciousness of the animals in my part of the world on a regular basis—elk, turkeys, ravens, foxes, and bobcats who also make their home in these mountains. Doing so gives me an expanded perspective on life, and a greater appreciation of the incredible ecosystem in which I live.

1. As you go about your day, pay attention to other forms of life. What creatures do you see on a regular basis?

2. Notice if one particular creature draws your attention—the bird that lives in the tree outside your house, or the spider spinning a web between the leaves of your houseplant.

3. When you spot this creature, allow yourself to slow down and pay close attention to it. Watch it for as long as you can. Use a set of binoculars, a magnifying glass, or even the zoom feature on your phone or camera to see it in more detail. Study its ways. Pay attention to any sounds or movements it makes. What is this creature doing? How is it interacting with its environment? What does it need to be happy and healthy?

4. Ask permission from the animal to enter its consciousness. This is very important. If it says "yes," you can proceed. If it says "no," you must not continue under any circumstances. Just move on to another creature.

5. If the creature grants its permission, intend for yourself to enter into its consciousness with an act of will. What does the world look like from this creature's perspective? What does it feel like to be so tiny, or so big? What does it feel like to have wings? Claws or scales? Multiple sets of arms and legs? To what is this creature exquisitely attuned? The fine vibrations of sound? The subtle scents of its food source?

Tiny changes in temperature? Imagine yourself being just as attuned to those things.

6. Imagine what it would feel like to move in the way this creature moves—to crawl slowly, one delicate leg at a time; or to slither through the grass with the sun on your back. Imagine what it would be like to find your food the way this creature does—by hunting for insects or foraging for seeds. Allow yourself to enter fully into this creature's experience, shedding as much of your human perspective as you can. What is its special medicine? Does it have a song to share with you?

7. When you feel complete, use that same intention to step out of the creature's consciousness. Make sure to bless it and perhaps leave a small offering as a sign of appreciation for it having shared its consciousness with you.

Repeat this practice as often as you like, going deeper and deeper into the consciousness of your chosen creature, or getting to know different forms of life.

The Extraordinary Practice
of Singing to the Land

In the mid-1990s, I went to my very first ayahuasca ceremony in the upper Amazon region of Peru. This traditional ceremony, which uses a psychoactive brew to support spiritual transformation, divination, and healing, took place on an island in a river that is one of the main headstreams of the Amazon. We sat in a clearing in the forest, a full moon bathing us in otherworldly silver light. One of the shamans leading the ceremony was a Shipibo woman who was known throughout the region and even throughout Peru as a highly skilled and knowledgeable singer of *icaros*, the beautiful, birdlike songs sung during these ceremonies. Shamans receive these songs as gifts from Spirit.

I was lucky enough to sit right next to this shaman during the ceremony. As the night wore on, I began to see the words of her songs coming out of her mouth in the form of visual patterns and lights that, combined with the sound of the melody she was singing, seemed to contain a force of love and wisdom that transcended the borders of language. These songs were filled with pure healing energy, and I knew from that moment that I was in the presence of a true master, someone with much to teach. Over the next few years, this woman helped me to find my own voice, and eventually taught me many icaros, which I still sing in ceremonies to this day.

Spiritual traditions around the world recognize the power of music to transform consciousness, promote community bonding, and heal the heart, mind, and body. Zen practitioners chant sutras; Christians sing hymns; shamans play drums and shake rattles to induce trance states. Music loosens the grip of our analytical, overthinking left brain nudging us into our holistic, creative right brain—a boon to any sort of spiritual practice and a strong medicine against anxiety, depression, and other ailments. I've come to believe that music is a form of alchemy—a portal straight to the heart of the divine.

Throughout most of human history, singing was a far more common feature of everyday life than it is today. People sang as they harvested crops, as they hoisted sails, and as they performed all types of repetitive manual labor. They also sang and danced for entertainment, to mark special occasions, and to connect with the divine. With the advent of recorded music, however, spontaneous and informal singing has become far less common. Today, we are much more likely to put on a favorite album than to sing ourselves. As a result, although there's nothing wrong with recorded music, we miss out on the joy of stretching our lungs, opening our hearts, and joining our voices in song.

Although I used to be quite shy about my voice, I now sing every day. I sing when I'm in ceremony, when I make offerings, and when I'm hiking in the mountains. Singing relieves muscle tension, promotes deep breathing, and has even been shown to boost the immune system. And whether we sing solo or in groups, our bodies release endorphins that can leave us feeling happier all day. Best of all, singing reminds us that our essential nature is peaceful, loving, and joyous.

Practice: Blessing Through Song

This practice shows you how to use the joy of singing to bless a place that is sacred to you. Just as the Earth Mother responds well to being greeted, she loves being sung to as well. She may even reward you with an unexpected rush of wind, a sudden flight of birds, the appearance of wildlife, or a distant roll of thunder showing that she has received your song.

> 1. Go to your favorite place in nature, whether that's a high mountaintop overlooking a winding river, or the oak grove in your local park.

If you like, you can bring a rattle, a drum, or another musical instrument.

2. Offer this place a song. You can use a song that you know, or you can sing, or hum, or even whistle spontaneously, creating a simple melody in response to what you see and feel.

3. If you're not ready to sing right away, begin by shaking your rattle or playing your drum until a song emerges naturally. Don't force anything. Be patient and allow the melody with or without words to reveal itself.

4. If possible, choose a simple tune with a repeating refrain—one you can sing over and over, gaining confidence as you go. You can also repeat a word or a simple phrase, for instance: "Blessings to you" or "River, you are my friend." Repetitive songs have a special ability to pull you into a gentle trance state in which you can forget your concerns and sink into relationship with whatever is right there with you, right now. You can hum or sing in any language. I like to sing in Spanish, because it opens my heart more readily.

5. Continue to sing until you feel that you have truly arrived in the place where you are sitting or standing—when you feel that you have connected with the place and perceive that it has noticed your presence and connected with you.

6. When you feel complete, finish your song and close your ritual by putting a hand on your heart, bowing, or making an offering—any gesture that feels significant to you.

PART FOUR

Physical Practices

Sometimes, the most effective way to elevate your consciousness is with practices that focus on the body. The body is a portal to the divine—a mysterious temple with endless wisdom for those who know how to unlock it. For this reason, spiritual traditions from shamanism to Christianity have all included physical practices. The body is also where we store all of our emotions. By working with the body directly, instead of staying on the level of conscious thought and language, we can process grief and trauma, freeing up trapped energy that can then be put to other uses. I try to incorporate at least one physical practice into my daily life, and I encourage my students to do the same.

The Extraordinary Practice
of Taking a Cold Shower

When I was a graduate student, I attended a workshop in which each participant had to take six glasses of ice-cold water and pour them down his or her back. I'll never forget the shrieks and laughter that filled the room as we all felt the shock of freezing water running from our brain stems down to our coccyx, an extraordinarily stimulating and refreshing process that brought on a warm afterglow.

Immersion in cold water is a classic technique for strengthening concentration. One American monk writes of an intense Zen retreat he attended that involved taking icy showers several times a day. He soon realized that the only way to make it through the experience without suffering was to embrace it completely, paying total attention to the cold. Taking a cold shower or plunging in a cold pool can also teach you self-discipline and help you overcome your addiction to comfort. Your body will usually acclimate itself to the experience within ten days, after which you will start to look forward to the process. And you will actually miss the feeling once you get used to it.

Exposing yourself to cold water is also a time-tested way to improve your body's health and vigor. Whether you step under a freezing waterfall or plunge into a cold pool after a hot sauna, it can release endorphins, reduce inflammation, and improve circulation. When I used to go to Finland to teach, smoke saunas were very popular. After enjoying the heat of the sauna, I was encouraged to plunge into a hole cut in the ice of a frozen lake. I thought I would die of the cold, but it actually felt very good afterward and I felt great for the rest of the day.

I learned more about cold dunking in Ecuador where, accompanied by my daughter, I visited a small town at the foot of an active volcano near the Amazon jungle. The village was home to thermal hot springs, which were close to an ice-cold pool. All the old-timers moved back and forth between the ultra-hot waters of the springs and the freezing cold waters of the pool. They advised us to spend five minutes in each and to make sure that we frequently dunked our heads under the water. While this was very tough to do because we were new to the practice, we managed to comply—with excellent results.

While on an eleven-day rafting trip on a river in Alaska, we wore wetsuits every day. After a time, of course, we had to bathe and the only choice was the frigid river, which had ice chunks floating down it. One by one, we took turns jumping in naked and screaming, immersing ourselves in the freezing water. Again, the results were fabulous.

How can something that feels so bad be so good for us? The key lies in a phenomenon known as *eustress,* which means, literally, "good stress." Eustress consists of challenging yourself just enough that you feel a sense of pride and amazement when you prevail, without seriously depleting your mental and physical resources. And cold-water showers are an easy way to experience this. Exposing yourself to the temporary shock and discomfort of a cold shower is indeed stressful—but the physical benefits and the thrill of overpowering your hesitations vastly outweigh the downsides.

My shamanic teachers have told me that, as we grow older, it's important to raise the bar on the challenges we accept. Old age is not the time to go easy on yourself. Indeed, you need to be tough if you're going to survive into your eighties, nineties, or beyond! This is one of the reasons I now take a cold shower every single day. Exposing myself to cold water wakes me up, challenges me, and keeps me fresh and vigorous.

Practice: Taking the Plunge

NOTE: If you are suffering from a cold or the flu, have an injury, have undergone recent surgery, or have certain health conditions, I don't recommend this practice.

Assuming you are basically healthy, you can take a cold shower every day to train the physiology of your body, increase your vitality, and strengthen your immune system. This very brief—but very potent—practice takes only three to five minutes a day—unless you are doing a complete scrub-down.

1. Begin by taking a warm shower and washing as usual. I have found that, before you turn on the cold water, it is best turn the hot water off completely so that you start with totally cold water. Starting with lukewarm water and slowly adding cold will not train your physiology in the same way. The trick to taking a cold shower is not to think at all; just "take the plunge," so to speak. Reach for the handle, turn off the warm water, and turn on the cold water without a thought.

2. Once you've switched to cold water, don't turn on the hot water again, because that defeats the purpose. Build up your tolerance

gradually—perhaps starting with thirty seconds and adding another fifteen seconds each day until you reach five minutes or so.

3. I usually start with the cold pouring over just my head, then my shoulders and the front of my body, and then exposing my back to lessen the shock. Finally, I let the cold water pour down the back of my head onto my brain stem and then all the way down my vertebrae. You can simply move your body forward and back to get the same effect I got using the glasses of ice water I mentioned earlier. This part is very important, because it stimulates the entire nervous system in a good way.

4. Keep your mind as empty as possible as you do this. Just feel the sensation of cold on your skin. Remember, cold is just an idea. We were taught that it is uncomfortable. But what if you looked forward to it instead? You can retrain your mind. Make the cold your ally. I have learned to make friends with the cold by thanking it for the benefits it gives me while it is pouring down.

5. When you are ready, turn the water completely off and enjoy the feeling of stimulation. Notice how you actually feel *warm*. Remember that the first few times are the hardest. After that, your physiology takes over and learns the new routine. Enjoy.

The Extraordinary
Practice of Fasting

When I was fourteen years old, I was part of a group that was inducted into the honor society of the Boy Scouts of America. As part of our initiation, we were required to spend twenty-four hours alone in the mountains of Southern California without anything to eat or drink. I remember being so excited about the adventure that I didn't really mind not eating—the hard part was not drinking water in the scorching California sun. At the end of the fast, I felt a tremendous sense of pride, along with a new appreciation for silence and solitude. I felt that I had scratched the surface of something very powerful, something I would be drawn to explore not just once, but again and again.

Much later, in my thirties, I did my first weeklong fast as part of a vision quest. This time, I was all alone on a beach in severe heat, with only silent cacti and buzzing rattlesnakes for company. Despite the hardship, I loved the experience. The fasting brought up deep feelings of grief and sorrow that I had been carrying around for years. I sat on that beach and sobbed. Afterward, I felt so light and free that I sang for hours. At the end of seven days, I didn't want to start eating again, nor did I want to break my solitude.

The practice of fasting is as old as the hills, and its benefits are legendary. The Buddha fasted under the bodhi tree until he was awakened, refusing all earthly sustenance. Jesus fasted for forty days and forty nights in a cave in the desert to free himself from his inner demons. Most of the great Hindu mystics and Tibetan lamas spent time fasting, and their present-day counterparts still do. From the rainforests of Peru to the mountains of New Mexico to the coasts of Labrador, shamanic peoples have always practiced fasting as a way to restore health to their bodies, bring clarity to their minds, and deepen their connection with the divine.

When we fast, our bodies take a break from the energy-intensive process of digestion and metabolism and put that energy to other uses. Our minds become sharper. Although sometimes we experience an initial emotional turbulence, a stillness eventually descends, and we can more easily access the spiritual states that often elude us in our everyday lives. In the words of Mahatma Ghandi: "Fasting leads to wisdom, wisdom leads to love, love leads to purity, and purity leads to God."

Fasting triggers a physical response called *autophagy*, in which your body starts breaking down and recycling old cell components. Although your body is always trying to make the most of the energy available to it, autophagy kicks that efficiency up a notch, converting weak or damaged materials into fresh, healthy cell components. At the same time, you may find that you go through a similar process on an emotional level while fasting—breaking down old patterns of resistance, resentment, and clinging, and releasing them at last. Although this can initially make you feel cranky or overwhelmed, it tends to resolve itself into a wonderful state of clarity and inner peace.

In some ways, fasting and dieting are similar. The difference is that, when you are on a diet, you usually eat a specialized selection of foods and cut back on other foods to provide you with specific benefits—for instance, losing weight or bulking up on muscle. In the Amazon jungle, where I usually go twice a year to diet with special plants under the supervision of the Shipibo shamans, the focus is more spiritually oriented. Specific plants give special qualities of protection or enhance specific abilities like clairsentience or clairaudience. Some plants provide healing or give the power to heal others. Many of the plants deliver teachings and provide quite elaborate visions. But that is another matter.

On a physical fast, you basically refrain from eating *all* foods and usually drink only water. On a spiritual fast, water is often denied as well. This is the case in Native American vision quests that usually last four days and nights. The fasting practice below includes drinking water, juice, or herbal teas so that you remain hydrated, which is better for your body. Hard-core fasts that restrict all liquids may not be as good for the body, although they can support other goals like discipline, the appearance of visions, and the weakening of the ego.

For some, fasting is not at all recommended. For example, if you have or have had an eating disorder, are pregnant or nursing, or are under eighteen years old, you should stay away from fasting because these are more complex situations that still have many unknowns. And while fasting can help decrease blood glucose levels, fasting generally isn't recommended if you have been diagnosed with diabetes.

If you have hypoglycemia, low blood sugar can leave you feeling tired and weak. It can also stimulate sleep disruptions. Some research has shown that fasting can lead to muscle loss. Gender may play a role in this as well, especially if you are deficient in minerals and other requirements. Research on blood sugar suggests that fasting can improve blood sugar in men, but that it made blood sugar levels worse in many women. Since our overall research-based knowledge is constantly evolving, you may want to check on the very latest information and recommendations before you start a fast.

Because of their more complex physiology, women may have more reasons to avoid severe fasting. Because of the impact fasting can have on hormones, women may experience more acute effects. Mood swings, missed or irregular periods, and, in extreme cases, fertility issues can be linked to hormonal shifts and stressors to the body (of which fasting can be one). If you are already highly stressed, adding fasting to the mix can be too much for the body to handle. And if you want to get pregnant or are already pregnant, fasting is not recommended.

For a fast that lasts longer than twenty-four or forty-eight hours, it helps to begin to restrict your food the day before you start the fast. Ceasing your food intake abruptly can be a little traumatic, and this helps prepare your body and mind gradually. In fact, I recommend talking to your body in advance and telling it what the plan is so that it feels included in the preparations. Remind yourself that you are choosing the experience of fasting, including the uncomfortable parts, knowing that the benefits will be worth it. Imagine your body getting a wonderful rest from the hard work of digestion, and your mind having the time and space to finally process stale emotions. Make your fast an experience of conscious celebration.

If you are new to fasting, start with a twenty-four-hour fast. If that goes well, you can gradually extend to longer fasts. Everyone's needs are a little different, so there are no set rules, but you can usually get all the benefits from a fast in four days and nights, or ninety-six hours. On the other hand, going up to five days or limiting yourself to three days may be what's best for you. Fasts lasting longer than five days and nights may teach you something valuable or help you in very specific ways, but you generally won't get any greater physical benefits from longer fasts. In fact, your body may begin to starve itself, and that is not necessary or beneficial.

People who elect to do long fasts usually include some ways of keeping their blood sugar up, like drinking juices or eating some fruits along the way. Again, you may choose to drink herbal tea or hydrate in the way that works best for you.

Another very important consideration is to maintain your electrolytes and keep mineral balances up in the body. Even on a short fast of four days, this is very important, because you can throw your body out of whack if you don't know what you are doing. Be sure to take some liquid minerals and electrolytes along with you on your fast, especially in hot weather.

Practice: Renewing Yourself Through Fasting

When you are fasting, don't attempt to carry your regular work load or do any hard exercise or labor. Set aside time for your fast and provide yourself with a setting and schedule that does not include any social obligations or demands. Shut off your phone, restrict all media and screens, and don't speak to anyone if you can help it. Don't check your texts, e-mails, or news feeds, and be sure to stay off all social media. Ideally, just let people know that you will be offline for three or four days.

For these reasons, many elect to get out of their usual surroundings and retreat to a private space to fast. See if you can use someone's cabin in the woods or an empty guest house for a time. An Airbnb in country surroundings works well too. You can fast in your own home if you have privacy and the discipline not to get distracted. In good weather, some people go to a beautiful place with a tent and just camp out.

Make sure you have privacy and an easy return trip home when your fast is over, because you may not have much energy. During the day, you can do some light yoga, Qi Gong, or Tai Chi. You can meditate at various times, or just keep a meditative attitude throughout. Just make sure you keep thinking and problem-solving to an absolute minimum. In fact, try fasting not just from foods, but from thinking, worrying, and reasoning. Try to be conscious and aware only of your perceptions and your sensations without indulging in judgments or considerations.

Accept your moods, your feelings, your mental state, and the way your body is responding. Keep as neutral as you can, and when your mind fixates on problems, work with the phrase: "Oh, is that so?"

Some find abstaining from food to be a very emotional experience. If you find yourself feeling anxious, weepy, irritated, or forlorn, simply hold those feelings with as much love as you can. Know that these feelings are revealing themselves to you because they are ready to be released. Fasting is detoxifying and sometimes that is uncomfortable, especially during the first twenty-four hours.

Above all, I suggest prayer. For spiritual purposes, fasting and prayer go hand in hand. Spend your time in gratitude, with love, and in awe as much as you can. Talk to Spirit at great length. Pour out your heart and spend some of your time listening to what comes into your mind as a result of your prayers.

I also recommend reading inspirational material and avoiding disturbing novels and reading that unsettles the mind and heart. For example, do not select a book about the impact of climate change on the planet to read during your fast. I highly recommend books by Paul Selig, Rupert Spira, Tom Kenyon, Pema Chödrön,

Adyashanti, Tulku Urgyen Rinpoche, and Yogananda, or you can choose books by your own favorite teachers. You can also listen to podcasts, lectures, and audiobooks.

Listening to music can be helpful, but make sure it is music that is conducive to peacefulness and keeping an open heart. Hard rock, hip hop, and techno are not the right kinds of music for fasting. Music without words is best.

Go to sleep when you feel like it. Wake when you want to. You do not have to keep the same old schedule. Break things up a bit. Overall, enjoy your fast. Decide when it will be over and stick to that schedule. Don't make your fast open-ended. When you come to the end of your fast, make some ritual gesture to acknowledge that it is over. For example, you can light incense, shake a rattle, or take a deep bow and say a few words of gratitude.

Break your fast with light foods like cucumbers or grapes—don't rush out to the diner and order a full breakfast! Give your metabolism time to wake up again. Notice if your body is craving healthier foods than it was before.

Healthy eating is always a key factor. Some think that they can eat whatever they want during eating times because they're fasting, but this is absolutely false. Don't pile on the deserts. Choosing healthy foods—including lots of fruits and vegies, whole grains, lean proteins, and lots of water—is still essential.

While it is one of the more physically challenging practices in this book, you may find that you enjoy fasting so much that you look forward to doing it every couple of months. There is no reason that fasting cannot become a regular part of your life. Everybody needs some break in their routine, and this is a highly beneficial way of getting one.

The Extraordinary
Practice of the Inner Smile

Ancient Taoist shamans of China understood the power of a smile. They knew that the simple act of smiling could have profound effects on our physical, emotional, and mental health, while extending benefits to everyone and everything nearby. They believed that the Tao—or Source—exists in a state of constant joy, and that when we smile along with the Tao, we align ourselves with its powerful healing energy. Likewise, the Toltecs speak of a "cosmic smile" that visits us in visions and dreams. For them, the most significant smiles are those bestowed upon us by toothless old crones. These grins are a sure sign that we're on the right path in our spiritual practice.

When you think about all the spiritual teachers who are frequently portrayed with a smile—Buddha, Quan Yin, and Krishna, to name a few—it becomes clear that smiling is an aspect of divinity. Smiles convey deep wisdom, compassion, and an enlightened state of being. The smiles of enlightened masters and avatars emerge naturally from their realization of oneness with all. They seem to embody a state of being in which fear, anger, and anxiety simply cannot exist.

Modern science confirms that when we smile, our bodies release endorphins and other feel-good chemicals even when we don't know what we are smiling about. When we smile, we tell our nervous systems: "Everything's alright. You're safe, protected, and beloved." Our nervous systems respond by relaxing. Our bodies soften, and we shift out of fight-or-flight mode. Studies have found that people who smile enjoy better friendships and relationships, report less stress in their day-to-day lives, and are overall more successful than people who smile less frequently.

Practice: Cultivating Your Inner Smile

This practice has its roots in the philosophy of Taoist sages, who believed that cultivating a gentle inner smile led to a long life and optimal health. Working with this practice every day makes me feel accepting, peaceful, and happy. I hope it will do the same for you.

1. Sit or stand in a posture you find comfortable.

2. Close your eyes halfway and allow a subtle, Mona Lisa–like smile to arise on your lips. As

you do this, smile with your heart, allowing yourself to feel grateful, beloved, and joyful. Feel how this inner smile spreads a beautiful radiance throughout your entire body.

3. Let your inner smile touch your heart, your stomach, your lungs, and any other organs you can think of. Let it touch any sore muscles or areas of pain, saturating them with its warmth and radiance. Hold the area of pain or discomfort in this loving energy until you feel it start to relax.

4. Let this inner smile saturate your mind. If you have any worries or mental tension, bathe them in the light and warmth of this smile until they, too, begin to relax.

5. Send your inner smile toward all beings on the planet. Imagine every living being sharing in the love, joy, and gratitude you feel right now.

6. If you are so inclined, you can gradually begin to contemplate more challenging topics. Try smiling with your lips and your heart while visualizing a person with whom you are in conflict, or an illness or disappointment, or

global conditions like climate change, poverty, war, inequality, or tyranny. But don't overdo it.

7. If you feel overwhelmed, return to more benevolent subjects like pets, loved ones, and nature. Tackle the harder topics *poco a poco*, gradually, with love in your heart. Not only will you become less triggered by them, you will subtly transform the world in a good way. This is excellent practice.

The Extraordinary Practice
of Shamanic Breathing

All around us, every day, everything that is alive is breathing. Flowers are breathing; trees are breathing; mosquitoes are breathing; all of your brothers and sisters here on earth are constantly breathing. Breath is the common denominator of all life. We all rely on clean air and healthy lungs, yet most of the time our bodies carry out this essential act below the level of our awareness. We forget that we are breathing; we forget that other life forms are breathing as well. And we forget that the air we share connects us to all life forms and makes us one.

The way we breathe has a significant impact on our mental health and overall well-being. This fact has been known by shamans, yogis, and sages since the beginning of time. Indeed, the first instruction in a wide range of spiritual practices consists of either learning how to bring awareness to the breath, or learning how to breathe in a different way. Practitioners of hatha yoga are instructed to "send" their breath to various parts of the body, particularly areas of pain. Zen students count their breaths. Shamans use deep, rhythmic breathing to enter a trance state.

In recent years, scientists have shed a lot of light on the exact mechanisms of this process. For example, research has found that deep breathing reduces the stress hormones adrenaline and cortisol, and may even assist the body in releasing antibodies, which strengthens our immune response. When we take slow, deep breaths, we activate our parasympathetic nervous system, which sends the body into a state of relaxation in which it can heal and recover from stress. There are also benefits to holding our breath for short periods of time—up to ten minutes—to increase our carbon dioxide tolerance and improve lung capacity.

The shamanic breathing practice that follows involves repetitive cycles of deep breathing, alternating with brief periods of holding your breath. By alternating between these two states, you can capture a wide range of physical, mental, and emotional benefits, putting yourself in an optimal state to go about your day.

You can do this practice anytime that works for you. I tend to do it first thing in the morning because I like to start my day with a full load of oxygen. Obviously doing it in a well-ventilated room is best—or better yet, outside when weather and climate permit.

You should not do this practice if you have pneumonia, bronchitis, a lung infection, or any lung condition that requires you not to strain your lungs, like emphysema. If you are in doubt, check with your health practitioner.

Practice: Breathing into Life

This practice involves four rounds of deep breathing, consisting of fifty breaths each. I suggest you budget around twenty minutes for it. You can sit, stand, or lie down, but be sure to wear comfortable, nonrestrictive clothing and loosen any tight collars or belt buckles to make sure your throat and diaphragm can move freely. Throughout the practice, breathe in through your nose to stimulate the nerves that lead directly to your brain. Mouth breathing bypasses these nerves.

1. Fill your lungs completely, then release all the air through your mouth in one big whoosh.

2. Repeat this process fifty times. I usually count on my fingers to keep track, counting single breaths on my right hand and each group of five breaths on my left. This may sound overly simple, but I have found that, if you don't keep track of your breathing in some way, you can

quickly become confused and forget where you are in your count.

3. When you have completed fifty breaths, let the air out on the last breath and then relax all the way and stop breathing. By this time, you will have accumulated a lot of extra oxygen in your blood stream so you won't have to breathe. You may be surprised at how long you can just enjoy the oxygen and go without breathing—up to as long as ten minutes, but usually closer to two when you are beginning. When you feel the need to breathe building, simply relax and see if you can hold your breath a little longer.

4. When you cannot hold your breath any longer, take a slow, deep breath in through your nose and hold it to the count of fifteen, then let it out slowly.

5. You have now completed the first full round of shamanic breathing.

6. Repeat this process three more times. After two hundred breaths, you will find yourself in an altered state that may be accompanied by feelings of expansion, bliss, or deep inner

peace, similar to the runner's high experienced by athletes. If your eyes are closed (and I recommend it), you may feel or see a brightness all around you, even though the room may be totally dark.

7. Remain like this for a few more minutes in a state of contemplation. Then allow yourself to enjoy the benefits of a well-oxygenated body as you continue with your day.

Even though the results of this practice are very rewarding—feeling more alive, more focused, clearer— you may still resist doing it because it is mildly stressful. It requires discipline to continue and make progress. But the practice has many benefits. Some maladies that have not yet been healed may ultimately disappear. You may find that even though you are not doing it with any particular intention, very helpful processes take place anyway as a result of this daily rush of excess oxygen. People have been known to mitigate symptoms of Parkinson's disease, dementia, diabetes, and many other debilitating conditions simply by focusing on the breath.

Breathing exercises like this one are part of ancient yogic breathing and a practice called Tumo that is used to help Tibetan Buddhist monks tolerate extreme cold in the Himalayas. Tolerating carbon dioxide buildup is a great way for athletes to extend their tolerance in stressful competitions while maintaining a steady, slow breath.

The Extraordinary Practice
of Illuminated Walks

During the recent pandemic, I walked nearly every day, usually with my dog, Sancho. He's a big dog and needs a lot of exercise, so I walked anywhere from two to five miles a day on a network of trails in the foothills of the mountains near my home. Sancho kept me focused and present as he encountered people on the trail, greeted other dogs, and seemed to disappear for periods of time. There were many days when he kept me waiting at the end of the walk as he tried to prolong the fun. During these walks, I listened to the allies that are always with me and these practices were revealed to me in clear specific terms. Here I am passing them on to you.

Although we tend to associate the word "meditation" with sitting cross-legged on a cushion, preferably in a serene and sunlit meditation hall, walking meditation has been practiced by Buddhists for thousands of years. Not only does walking give the body a break from long hours of sitting in meditation, it helps to ward off the sleepiness that can often descend when we sit still. Moreover, it teaches us how to carry an enlightened mind out of the meditation hall and into the world.

Walking has a natural rhythm that can sink you effortlessly into a meditative state. As your arms and legs swing back and forth and your breathing automatically regulates, it becomes easier to quiet your chattering mind, allowing peace and wisdom to emerge. With the scenery flowing past and the fresh air touching your skin, feelings of gratitude and equanimity start to bubble up without any additional effort from you. The natural rhythms of walking can support spiritual awakening, and help you become a more expanded you—a you that is not separate and disconnected.

Walking to Awaken

Awakening to Spirit is very much like falling asleep when you are ready for bed. If you try to force yourself to go to sleep, you won't succeed. You just have to let go and fall asleep. And you can't force yourself to awaken, either. You just allow it to happen. The walking practices given below can revolutionize your conscious awareness and facilitate your spiritual awakening. It just takes practice—and that's why we do practices.

Contrary to much spiritual lore about people becoming self-realized in a sudden blinding flash, most of the time the process takes place poco a poco, little by little. The root of the word "grail" is the same as the root of the word "gradually," and the search for the Holy Grail was a metaphor for the gradual awakening of consciousness. This is not to say that people never experience a sudden awakening. They may, but it usually occurs after long practice. Siddhartha Gautama woke up only after many days and nights sitting under the bodhi tree, and many days of searching and wandering before that. Jesus spent forty days and forty nights fasting and praying in the desert, and years of training before that in preparation for his own awakening. People tend to forget that preparation and practice are key to enlightenment.

Sometimes the process is so gradual that we don't notice the exact moment when we awaken. Do you always know the second you are awake after a night of sleep? Probably not. I know I don't. Sometimes it is a slow dawning. Sometimes it happens more quickly.

The walks suggested below are spiritual practices, and in that sense they are not leisurely strolls or just opportunities to let your mind wander. Our monkey minds are often extremely active even when we are walking, and if we are not careful, our thoughts often become immersed in problems, tensions, and internal dialogues. As a result, instead of rejuvenating us, a walk can turn into a time of worry and displeasure.

Here, I suggest that you take charge when this happens and instead turn your walk into a practice that will leave you in a much more positive state of mind. The way out of suffering is often to get rid of the one who suffers. These practices do this both directly and indirectly, and they can also be fun and engaging. You will also find that they encompass some of the other practices included in this book, demonstrating how you can combine practices to get the most out of them.

Practice: Here, Now, New, Free, Be

Select a trail or walking route about a mile to three miles in length. Ideally, you should choose a trail to which you can return often, perhaps two or three times a week.

1. Begin your walk and maintain a leisurely pace. Inwardly say the word "here" every time you land on your right foot. Pay attention to being *here* each time you say it. You are always here, no matter how far you think you have walked.

2. Once you get the hang of this, add the word "now" every other time you land on your right foot. Each time you say "here," pay attention to being here, and each time you say "now," pay attention to being *present*. Keep up this cadence

of alternating between saying "here" and "now" each time your right foot hits the path.

3. After you have done this for a while, add the word "new" to the pattern. Realize that you are *brand new* each time you say it. You are here, you are now, and you are new.

4. Now add the word "free" to the pattern. When you say "free," contemplate that by being here, now, and new, you are truly *free*, with no past, no narrative to constrain you in any way.

5. Finally, add the word "be" to the pattern. When you say "be," contemplate that by being here, now, new, and free, you are in fact just *being* as you are, the only thing you can ever be, and thus you are in your true original nature.

6. Keep walking like this until you can no longer focus. If you lose your focus, pause, reset, and begin again or end the practice for the day.

Practice: Thinking and Being

This practice is a good way to release tension and free yourself from troubling thoughts.

1. As you begin your walk, review your troubles—perhaps an embarrassing moment at an office meeting where you were caught unprepared, or a conflict with a colleague who has been bothering you, or even a place where you always get stuck with your siblings and how you dread their calls.

2. Pick a trouble, ponder it, and try to solve the problem. Then take note of how you feel after about ten minutes of this. Did you resolve anything? Solve anything? Make any progress through the reasoning and thinking process?

3. Continue walking, but now try to keep your mind blank as much of the time as possible. Just notice the rhythm of your walking, the colors and textures on the trail, the smells, the sensations. When you go off into various thoughts, bring yourself back as quickly as you can to that empty-mind state of just being aware, of just being with the environment.

4. If you come across people, greet them normally and see if you can pass them without wondering about them or thinking about them beyond waving or saying hi.

5. At the end of your walk, notice how you feel. What is your state of mind? What was the general outcome of your walk? Which part of your walk did you enjoy more?

Practice: Divinity Walk

This practice can help you recognize the divine in yourself and in everything around you.

1. As you walk along the trail, say to yourself: "All is divine, as am I." Repeat this phrase like a mantra until you feel that you've "arrived" in a calm and benevolent state of awareness.

2. Allow yourself to feel the divinity in your footsteps, in the ground or pavement under your feet, and in the fresh air flowing into your lungs. Allow your gaze to soften and your mind to relax.

3. Continue to walk, realizing that the words "as am I" in your mantra do not refer to your little self, but rather to the Big Self, "the big I Am" — all that is included in consciousness, all that is present and aware throughout the universe.

4. When you feel ready, start introducing variations to this phrase. For example: "All is sacred, as am I." "All is blessed, as am I." "All is holy, as am I." "All is filled with love, as am I."

5. Notice the impact of these phrases on your awareness and your state of being. Do the colors of the trees and plants look more vibrant to you? Do the faces of the people you meet seem more welcoming and kind? What changes for you when you affirm the divinity in all things?

6. When you come to the end of your walk, bow to Spirit in everything or make some other gesture of gratitude. Carry the sense of divinity with you throughout the rest of your day.

Practice: Awareness Walk

Use this practice to raise your awareness of your higher self, and of your essence as a conscious being apart from your physical existence.

1. As you walk, ask yourself: "Am I alive? Am I conscious? Am I aware? Am I aware of my consciousness? Am I aware of my aliveness in this very moment? Am I aware of my awareness?"

2. Ask yourself: "Who is walking? Who is thinking? Who is feeling?"

3. Notice your sensations and perceptions—the feeling of your body walking; the sensations of your feet as they contact the ground; the sensations of heat or cold, sweat or goose bumps; the breeze on your skin and hair; the warmth of the sun.

4. Notice what you perceive with your eyes— bushes, trees, and rocks; fences and homes; flashes of sunlight through the branches of trees; the path moving beneath your feet; the perception that you are moving along a path or trail.

5. Pretend that you are wearing virtual-reality goggles and that all movement is an illusion. Your awareness is not going anywhere. You are staying still while your perceptions are changing. Stay with this experience as long as you can.

6. When you get back to the starting point of your walk, ask yourself: "Did my awareness really go anywhere at all?"

7. Consider the possibility that your awareness, your consciousness, never goes anywhere. It just records changing sensations and perceptions as they seem to pertain to the illusion of objects moving around a physical form that you identify as *you*. This physical form seems to be recording sensations about being a container of consciousness. Are these sensations, images, perceptions, and ideas the whole truth about who and what you are? Is there, in fact, a physical form with your name on it, or is it an elaborate and extremely believable hoax, ruse, or illusion?

Never agonize over these practices. If that starts to happen, stop them immediately and take a break, because you will get nowhere through agony and frustration. Come back to them when you can play a little more and when you find the process fascinating. You may feel discomfort, but you will soon realize that discomfort is a part of growing and it is exactly in alignment with Spirit. Then you will relax again.

The Extraordinary Practice of Finding Your Glad-to-Be-Alive Spot

Lying just beneath your sternum is your sinoatrial, or SA, node, which creates the electrical impulses that initiate your heartbeat. This tiny structure, no more than three millimeters wide and one millimeter thick, is the place where your will to be alive resides. Twenty-four hours a day, beginning before you were even born, your heartbeat has been powering your life. Even in moments when you're experiencing the depths of despair and don't know how to go on, your heart keeps beating, urging you to find a way.

My Toltec teachers call this area of the heart the "place of flowering." They say that when you focus your attention on this spot when praying or setting an intention, your prayers are supercharged with power. I've come up with my own name for it. I call it the "glad-to-be-alive spot." Even when I'm having a miserable day, there is something inside me that is always glad to be alive, and my heartbeat is proof of that fact. By maintaining an awareness of my heartbeat, I remember that I am here on earth for a reason, and that I can always respond to the events of my life with love.

Spiritual texts from around the world confirm the importance of the heart. In Hindu tradition, the heart chakra, known as *anahata*, is considered the center of love and compassion. Sufi mystics speak of the spiritual heart, or *qalb*, and consider it to be the organ for receiving divine grace. Their emblem is a heart with wings. I have referred to the qalb as the "heart of hearts," which has no physical location. Buddhist teachings encourage practitioners to cultivate loving-kindness and compassion from the heart center. In the Catholic tradition, Jesus and Mother Mary are both depicted pointing to their hearts, emphasizing where to find the kingdom of God. In Chinese medicine, the heart is believed to house the *shen*—the spirit or mind.

No matter which spiritual or philosophical framework you choose, you'll find that the heart is depicted as the core of our experience of being alive. In theosophy, this is the spot where the Creator fuels the body with truth (gold), love (rose), and energy (electric blue), the three building blocks of the universe. One famous picture of Jesus shows these three colors of light streaming out of his heart.

Practice: Linking Hearts

This practice can teach you to tune in to your heartbeat whenever you need reassurance that there is a part of you that is glad to be alive. And once you are in contact with that spot, you can link your own heartbeat to those of all living creatures who are likewise making their way on this earth.

1. Locate the sensitive spot in the center of your sternum and press lightly. Your sinoatrial node is located just beneath this spot. If you want to, you can massage this spot with your fingertips.

2. Bring your attention to this area and imagine that you can feel each heartbeat at its exact point of origination.

3. Realize that all the functions of your body depend on this spot continuously sending out life force.

4. Ask yourself where this life force comes from. What is this miraculous power that makes your heart beat?

5. Extend your awareness to the people you love. Just like you, their hearts are powered by this same mysterious force.

6. Extend your awareness to include every living being whose heart is beating right now—cats and dogs, butterflies and birds, snakes and fish—billions upon billions of hearts beating all over the earth.

7. Allow your heart to feel a sense of kinship with all these other hearts. Remember that, just like you, all of these billions of other beings want to be happy, healthy, and at peace. Recall that, just like you, all these other hearts are glad to be alive.

Return to the awareness of your heartbeat whenever you feel lost, overwhelmed, or alone. In fact, all you have to do is point to your heart and you will feel positive effects.

The Extraordinary Practice of Entering the Upper Room

The human brain contains four ventricles—open spaces into which the cerebrospinal fluid delivers nutrients and from which it takes away toxins. In alchemical, shamanic, and mystical circles, the third ventricle—enclosed by the diencephalon, located at the exact center of the brain—is known as an extremely powerful portal through which we can travel from lower levels of consciousness to higher ones. This ventricle is so central that some of the most important structures of the brain lie around it: the pineal and pituitary glands and the thalamus and hypothalamus surround it; the corpus collosum is right nearby, along with the hippocampus and the ocular nerve. In other words, it is right near the absolute center of our consciousness. In addition, it has a strong connection, through the brain stem and spinal cord, to our hearts—like a flower on top of a stem.

The Toltecs call this part of the brain the Black Eagle. The Wixarika call it the Mansion. Hindus call it the Cave of Brahma. The Buddha referred to it as Emptiness, and Tibetan Buddhists call it the Crystal Palace. The Shipibo call it el Templo, or the Temple, while mystics call it the Upper Room. Jesus referred to it as the Kingdom of Heaven. Yogic traditions call it the Third Eye, and it undoubtedly has many, many other names.

Mystics and shamans have long believed that by focusing your awareness on your third ventricle, you can access heightened spiritual states. For example, in his book *Kriya Yoga*, swami Paramahamsa Hariharananda wrote: "The longer you remain [in the third ventricle], the more you will hear a constant divine sound (aaahhhh) and feel a constant touch sensation of God and visualize an effulgent divine light that altogether will lead you to a blissful sojourn in the Kingdom of Heaven." In other yogic traditions, practitioners believe that when the third ventricle is activated during deep states of meditation, it secretes *amrita*—the "nectar of the gods"—which brings about feelings of bliss.

In the next three practices, you can learn to enter your own Upper Room to access states of wisdom, divine love, and deep inner peace. Knowing that this room is always available to you, you will be less perturbed by the ups and downs of everyday life. Setbacks and crises won't seem as devastating; material successes and outward wealth will become less important. Having discovered the riches of the Upper Room, you can expand and live from a place of service, devoting yourself to the well-being of the entire universe instead of only concerning yourself with your small, individual life.

Practice: Seeing Through Your Third Eye

Some students have told me that when they accessed their Upper Room using this practice, it washed away a lifetime of fear and anxiety, restoring them to the expansive state that is every human's birthright. This practice can help you "see" this state through your Third Eye.

1. Begin by saying the phrases: "All is sacred, as am I." "All is holy, as am I." "All is divine, as am I." "All is blessed, as am I." These phrases will put you in the proper mental and emotional space to do this work.

2. Close your eyes and roll them upward until you are looking a bit cross-eyed at the center of your forehead. Do not strain. With practice, you can do this with your eyes open.

3. Focus your attention between the tips of your ears, where the third ventricle is located. Enter the ventricle and imagine that it is a comfortable little cavelike room where you can hang out for a bit. This is "command central"

for your brain, like the bridge of a ship. It is the safest and most powerful place your consciousness can reside. It is also completely neutral. Relax and just rest here for a couple of minutes.

4. Get used to spending time here. Practice opening your eyes as you are resting there. Do not rush out to meet whatever objects you see around you. Stay in the room and look out of your Third Eye as if it is a big window in front of you. This is the most powerful way of being, period. It will help you to stay neutral in any situation, to remain calm. It will help you stay in touch with your higher self.

Do this practice daily, and you will soon be able to access your Upper Room easily, anytime you like.

Practice: Spinning the Golden Egg

You can take the previous practice further by visualizing a golden egg standing upright and spinning very quickly counterclockwise within the third ventricle. As it spins, it will cleanse you of all negativity.

The spinning egg acts like a magneto to create a scalar wave, a toric field of great power and intensity, a radiating wave that moves out in every direction equally, until the bottom of it reaches just below your heart and is equidistant in every direction around your head. This golden field surrounding your head and upper chest creates a sense of calm, tranquility, serenity, and neutrality. It is the halo seen in depictions of saints from all traditions. You can experience this for any time period and it will feel very good.

Practice: Entering the Upper, Upper Room

This practice is actually very simple, but profound in its implications. Once you get the hang of it you will no longer need to enter, because you will be there all the time. This takes a lot of practice, but it is worth every moment.

While in the Upper Room, close your eyes and imagine that there is a little stair or ladder in front of you that leads up to a trapdoor or opening in the ceiling. Approach the ladder or stair and climb the three or more steps up until your head and perhaps your shoulders as well emerge into the upper space.

This upper space may look different to different people, but it tends to have several general characteristics: It is lit by a very bright, diffused light that comes from an unknown source. There are no objects present, and it seems to have no dimensions. It is not confined or delimited by walls, a ceiling, or even a floor. It is boundless and eternal.

This space is not in the physical universe. It exists outside of time and space, like the heart of hearts. It is a place of absolute peace and tranquility, and yet it may be filled with the most extraordinary vitality and fertility. The amplitude of the vibrations in this space is so high that it is impossible to feel any fear or anxiety, any discouragement or depression. It is a higher dimension, a higher octave available to human beings only if they can find their way here or are shown how to access it. Your experience here may be stunning and utterly transformative.

Your ego or false personality cannot enter here. It is a place you can only enter on an essence level. So the more often you go here, the more your essence self will take over your life. You will find only truth here, no lies or distortion.

This Upper, Upper Room is a portal to other dimensions, an entrance to the spirit world, to the kingdom of heaven. Anything you want to banish can be lifted into this space, where it will be subject to the highest vibration and obliterated or transformed into something of a higher purpose. This is the end of fear—if you can stay here. Here in this space, there is no narrative, no thought, none of the usual mind chatter, just a feeling of being stabilized and neutral and blissful.

Accessing the Upper, Upper Room takes daily practice, but not through effort or struggle. Rather, it just requires attentiveness and focus at various times of the day for a few seconds here and there.

The Extraordinary Practice
of the Singing Shaman

The practice of the singing shaman is represented in ancient statues that have been unearthed and discovered in various places on the planet, attesting to how widespread this practice has been from ancient times. It is a simple but powerful practice that opens the lungs and the heart and gives voice through the throat. It may open centers throughout the whole body. Certainly it increases circulation and alters your state of consciousness in a wonderful way. You can expect to feel more expansive, inspired, bright, and clear after performing it, and these feelings will remain with you for hours.

Practice: Singing into Power

This practice, which is based on more current similar shamanic practices, teaches you to open and build power that can be used for healing, ceremonies, and rituals. It is best done outdoors, but if that is not convenient you can do it anywhere you have a little privacy. It is also dramatically more powerful if a group of people do it together, perhaps standing in a circle or, if it is a larger group, just standing together. When performed by a group, it can often be done for longer periods of time.

1. Stand erect with your heels together but with your feet angled out in a forty-five-degree V shape.

2. Keep your knees slightly bent and your body relaxed but upright, with your head balanced and facing slightly upward.

3. Make loose fists of your hands and hold them against your sternum in a similar forty-five-degree V shape, with the knuckles of your little fingers touching and your thumbs resting on your index fingers, which are folded inward with the rest of your fingers.

4. Keep your thumbs three to four inches apart. This is the exact position you would use to open your coat by the lapels or that Superman would use to reveal his costume underneath his shirt when he is about to fly off on some mission.

5. Open your mouth and sing "aaaaahhhhhhhh" for as long as you can, until your breath runs out. Then breathe in through your nose rather quickly and repeat so that it is like one long, stretched-out sound lasting several minutes.

6. When you are finished, simply stand and feel into whatever you experience in silence. For some, this is the time of greatest discovery. For others, the whole process may include visions, impressions, perceptions, revelations, emotions, and other possible responses. If you are working in a group, you can share your experiences at this time.

I find this to be a very powerful practice when I am out hiking or by myself for several days.

PART FIVE

Creative Practices

Creative practices are ubiquitous in spiritual traditions from around the world. For example, in Hinduism, visualizing the face of a beloved guru is believed to be an important way of calling in that person's wisdom, love, and guidance. In Buddhism, practitioners spend hours imagining a particular deity in extraordinary detail, seeing that deity's clothing and jewelry and the exact position of their fingers and toes. In hatha or kundalini yoga practice, people sometimes imagine colored light at the position of their chakras, with the purpose of strengthening or healing those areas.

Creativity is at the heart of the shamanic tradition as well. I have witnessed shamans performing extractions in a great variety of ways in different parts of the world. Shipibos in the Amazon use tobacco, while the Wixarika prefer feathers and blessed water. Aboriginals in Australia simply use their hands to extract illness and disease. The ayahuasqeros of Peru hardly ever sing their icaros the same way or with the same words twice. Their pitch and even the melody may change during a song.

Regardless of your faith or spiritual tradition, harnessing your own creativity is a powerful way to access deep experiences of inspiration, connection, forgiveness, healing, and love.

The Extraordinary Practice of Glowing Like the Sun

When I was in my early thirties, I began to study Qi Gong—the ancient Chinese practice of cultivating the subtle energies of the body through movement, breathwork, and meditation. The ancient Taoists who developed Qi Gong believed that human beings could absorb the energy of the sun and moon (qi) for optimal health and well-being, and this belief is reflected in the beautiful names of their exercises: "hugging the moon," "gathering the moon qi," "absorbing qi from the sun."

But the Taoists weren't the only ones to believe that human beings could improve their health and vitality by connecting to celestial bodies. In shamanic cultures, shamans "charge" their drums, rattles, crystals, feathers, and other sacred tools by bathing them in the light of the full moon or the rising sun. Yogis do daily rounds of sun salutations. Christians attend midnight Mass around the time of the winter solstice, and sunrise Mass at Easter to mark the triumph of life over death. The

Wixarika gather the power of the sun with their feathers as it shines through the core of the earth at midnight to heal and energize their compadres.

Just as the sun's warmth and light causes seeds to sprout and crops to grow, we all have an inner sun that can support our spiritual journey if we know how and when to focus its light. By seeing this inner sun in all its radiance, we can invoke its qualities of warmth, light, and healing, flooding ourselves with the strength we need to overcome our own battles with darkness. Although most people experience sadness, depression, or ill health from time to time, connecting with your inner sun can help you move out of these states quickly, returning to the health and harmony that is your natural state.

Practice: Harnessing the Power of Your Inner Sun

This practice teaches you how to harness the power of creative seeing to flood your body with the wonderful, healing light of your inner sun. By imagining your inner radiance glowing out from every cell of your body, you supercharge your ability to heal from illnesses, recover from stress, and keep a positive mindset.

1. Pick any location in your body—a fingertip, a toe, your heart, your sternum, your liver.

2. Imagine that you have a powerful electron microscope that allows you to focus in on a tinier

and tinier area of that body part, until you have zoomed in on a single cell and then a single atom of that cell.

3. Imagine that this single atom starts to glow from the inside, and that you can control the brightness of that glow with a little dimmer switch.

4. As you raise the dimmer switch, the light becomes brighter. Soon, it becomes so bright that it is hard to look at—like a miniature sun. The brightness spreads to the surrounding atoms and they all start to glow as you raise the switch on the dimmer.

5. Zoom out slowly with your microscope and see this light spreading out to include the whole cell and then gradually through all the cells in your body, until your entire body is glowing intensely.

6. Feel yourself glowing with benevolence, love, and good health. Feel this healing light radiating out to bless all those around you.

7. When you feel complete, lower the dimmer switch until your body returns to its normal light level.

The Extraordinary Practice of Claiming the Highest Possibility for Your Life

I first learned about attracting the highest possibility of my life from studying Toltec techniques to exchange lesser probabilities for the greatest one. According to the Toltecs, your greatest possibility is related to your navel, which in turn is related to the Earth Mother—whom we might call Mother Nature or Mother Earth, and the people of the Andes and the Amazon call Pachamama. For them, the Earth Mother is the source of all largess, all prosperity, all success. The Toltecs believe that she is a face of Spirit, an expression and representative of the Creator, so to speak, and their mythology makes this very clear. So, in order to prosper, to become abundant, and to realize our greatest potential in this life, we must have a good, strong relationship with Pachamama. When we do, she will provide for our every need.

According to the Toltecs, because of where we are in their calendar system and prophecies, now is the perfect time to reestablish our relationship with the Earth Mother, who, in many ways, is more reliable as a mother. In order to do this, we need to refocus on the navel area, and reestablish and strengthen our inner umbilical cord that connects us to the earth. This inner umbilical cord, which is invisible to the naked eye, is our energetic link to Pachamama, a link that has become weakened and diminished by our neglectful lifestyles.

The Toltecs of ancient Mexico believed that we all have a highest possibility that can be ours if we have the vision, skill, and courage to claim it. This highest possibility is not set in stone, but changes from moment to moment depending on the decisions we make and the actions we take. For example, when you are twenty years old and unattached, your highest possibility may be to live as a rebellious artist, completely outside the norms of society and beholden to no one except yourself. If you make the choice to get married and have children, your highest possibility will change in response to that choice. Perhaps it will become to teach your children to respect and care for the earth, so they can grow up to help adapt skillfully to climate change.

There are some good clues to indicate what this highest possibility may look like for each of us. You often gain a glimpse of your highest possibility as a child, but then, as you grow, you lose faith, you lose the dream and settle for much less. Try looking back at your childhood and remembering what your dreams were then, what you played at doing. Sometimes there are clues in how others see you or respond to you. Do others see you as a good storyteller? As organized, or coordinated, or funny? Do they see you as good with people? Or tenacious? Do they appreciate that you have an eye for balance and beauty, or excellent discernment? Do they find that you demonstrate leadership? Exhibit mastery? The list goes on and on.

Other clues can be found in what you enjoy doing. What is fun for you? What doesn't feel like work to you? What activities seem to open doors of opportunity for you? What serendipitous events seem to steer you in the right direction? These are all clues that can lead you to a realization of your highest possibility, to what shamans call your true medicine.

Your highest possibility is not necessarily correlated with the greatest material wealth or external success. Rather, it represents the highest expression of your values and talents at that particular moment. Moreover, your highest possibility is, by definition, possible. Although it may take work and perseverance to achieve, or even a few leaps of faith, it's not so difficult or outlandish that you can't achieve it.

In the following practice, you call on a spirit helper—in this case, a jaguar—to help you claim your highest possibility, no matter what the obstacles may be. By visualizing yourself being aided by a powerful helper like a jaguar, the internal and external obstacles that seem to stand between you and your highest possibility stop feeling so onerous, and you realize that reaching it isn't as hard as it looks.

Practice: Calling on Your Inner Jaguar

Before doing the practice, I recommend warming up a number of times over a few days or perhaps even regularly. The Toltecs suggest focusing on your navel area and getting in the habit of bathing it with golden energy, or light. According to them, the navel is the place where the "personal jaguar" lives in each of us. This will not only increase your success with this practice, it will endear you to this powerful ally.

1. Begin by imagining that there is a mountain in the distance. On top of that mountain is the place where your highest possibility resides. But between you and that peak there is a steep ridge covered in razor-sharp knives that you have to travel over on foot to reach the mountain. You would be cut to ribbons on your way there. But your ally the jaguar is magical and can fly anywhere you wish.

2. Ask the jaguar to fly you to the mountaintop to retrieve the latest version of your highest possibility for this lifetime. When she comes forward, climb on her back and grip her fur. She rises into the air and flies directly for the mountaintop in the distance—right over the ridge covered in sharp knives.

3. When you arrive and she lands, climb off her back and retrieve your highest possibility. This will be in the form of a symbol, like a sword, a basket, or a musical instrument.

4. Take a moment to contemplate the significance of this symbol. Allow a vision of your future self to pop into your head. What do you see yourself doing? Where are you? Who are you with?

5. Once you have retrieved your symbolic object, climb back onto your jaguar and ask her to fly you swiftly back. Don't expect the symbol to make total sense at first. It will reveal its true meaning over time.

6. You may have to do this practice a number of times over several weeks to retrieve all of your

symbol, and it is a good idea to return to the mountain periodically to get the latest version of it, because, as you develop your capacity, your highest possibility may grow bigger in ways that you did not expect.

7. Never fail to thank your jaguar for the flight to the mountain and back. With practice, your relationship with her will grow stronger and she may be able to help you in a variety of ways.

8. Your highest possibility is yours now. All you have to do is live it. Every day, visualize the symbol you retrieved from the mountaintop, and let it serve as motivation and inspiration for you to work toward your dream.

The Extraordinary
Practice of the Tree of Life

The Tree of Life is one of the great shamanic maps of the universe. The crown of the Tree—its branches and foliage—symbolizes the Upper World, the world of creativity and the future. It is like the head of the human body. The trunk of the Tree represents the Middle World that we occupy. It encompasses the present and is like the torso of the body. The roots of the Tree are the Lower World, where the past and lost knowledge reside. They are like the legs and feet of the human body.

Shamanic peoples all over the world honor the Tree of Life by decorating trees in the forest, leaving them offerings, and petitioning them with ceremonies. The trees people decorate at Christmas are a legacy of this historical shamanic understanding of the Tree of Life as a map. Moreover, the Tree of Life is associated with the other great shamanic map, the medicine wheel—which some see as a mandala-shaped slice taken out of the trunk of the Tree.

Practice: Linking the Earth Mother to the Cosmos

This simple practice shows you how to use the Tree of Life as a device for linking the Earth Mother to the cosmos, thereby unifying heaven and earth, earth and sky. It can also be used as a symbolic way to support the human body and its energy systems by facilitating the circulation of fluids in the body for greater health and vitality. You will actually feel this as you do the practice.

1. Imagine that there is a great column of light passing through your entire body. This light is the trunk of the great Tree of Life.

2. At the bottom of the column are four great roots that go in the four directions deep into the earth.

3. At the top of this great column, in the upper atmosphere of the planet, are four great branches that likewise go in the four directions. They all have beautiful foliage that faces the sun, the moon, the planets, and the stars, and all the heavenly bodies. These leaves are soaking up the relevant light codes from all over the cosmos and bringing them down through the

top of your head and all the way to the roots of the great Tree deep in the earth.

4. Meanwhile, the vitality, fertility, and information from the Earth Mother in the form of light is coming up from deep down in the earth. It radiates up through your navel and continues to rise up to the branches, where it is broadcast to the cosmos. This becomes a constant stream of light traveling in both directions, so that you become a means by which the Earth Mother speaks to the cosmos and the cosmos responds. You become the vital link that unifies them. At the same time, these currents are impacting and influencing your body, stimulating the rise of the cerebrospinal fluid coming up from the base of your spine to your brain and then back down again.

5. In return for this service you are performing—using your body as the Tree—the Earth Mother will take good care of you and will reward you with riches beyond anything you can imagine. Remember that her idea of riches encompasses much more than monetary gain. But if resources are what you need, she will provide them.

6. Accept your good fortune however it comes,
but don't abuse it or she will stop the flow.

This is one of the most practical and powerful practices I know of to transform your life experience from feeling trapped in the prison of self-limitation to absolute freedom to shine in your own light. It accomplishes this by cultivating your relationship with the Earth Mother, focusing on the navel area, and offering transformative actions using powerful symbols and allies to shift your experience.

The Extraordinary Practice of Beautiful Flowers Blossoming Within and Without

The Wixarika refer to themselves as "walking flowers." They dress very much like flowers, wearing colorful embroidered garments. Both men and women wear wide-brimmed hats topped with yarn in the shape of a peyote plant. They believe that we humans are already like flowers, and that we should emulate flowers and actively and creatively honor them. In modern times, powerful microscopes have revealed that deep within the cells of our bodies, there are brightly colored organelles that look remarkably like fields of flowers. Flowers are beautiful, and so are human beings when they operate out of essence.

It is readily apparent that we have much in common with flowers. We grow up toward the sun and develop a blossom (our brain) that blooms and radiates with light and joy. Eventually, that flower goes to seed and, after scattering our seeds (wisdom and learning) among the people, our bodies eventually wither and die, only to return to blossom again in each lifetime. We like to bask in the sun and let it shine on our faces. We need fertile ground to grow healthy and strong, and water to fuel our roots. We need sunlight to grow straight and tall. We are perfumed and come in many colors—red, brown, yellow, white, and black. Our hair radiates out like petals, and we fertilize each other to produce offspring.

Flowers carry a very high vibrational energy field. They lift us up and are great sources of inspiration. We love to cultivate them, gather them, and bring them into our homes to freshen the atmosphere and beautify the house for as long as they last. We wear them in our hair and in our lapels; we hold bouquets of them in our hands; we decorate our walls with paintings of them. We marry and die surrounded by flowers, and exchange bouquets of them during meaningful occasions like graduations, virtuoso performances, and completions. They are often at the center of our spiritual ceremonies and religious services, and hold the central position on altars and dining tables. In fact, flowers are so central to our lives that no one can imagine life without them.

Yet flowers don't actually *do* anything. They are excellent at just being present. And that is why we love them—because they teach us how to just *be*. They bring peace, joy, happiness, and beauty—all things to which we aspire in our lives. They are the perfect representatives of awareness, consciousness, presence, and life itself. You can't get much higher than that.

Flowers and beauty simply flow together. The Navajo and other indigenous tribes have a practice they call "the beauty way," a way of being that constantly refocuses them on all the beauty in life. They walk in beauty, work in beauty, sleep in beauty, and speak in beauty. Beauty lies before them, behind them, and to the right and left of them. Most important, they become aware of the beauty that resides within every human.

Awareness is Spirit, and Spirit is always beautiful. The more you cultivate beauty in your life, the more you align with the beauty that is already within you, and this awakens you in ways that are hard to describe. The more presence you manifest, the more beauty is revealed to you, and you begin to attract it from the environment all around. As a result, you become extremely attractive to other humans who dimly realize that what they crave is beauty, love, and aliveness. By walking in beauty, you show others a way to find that same beauty in themselves.

The Toltecs devised practices that use the beauty of flowers to lift us up and help us bring about those things we most want in our lives. Here is an example of a special practice that I have used many times to great advantage. It can change your life rapidly for the better in so many ways.

Practice: Walking in Beauty

Sometimes it is best to avoid words altogether and focus on an activity that involves powerful symbols of transformation. The Toltecs were experts at this, and their understanding of the power of flowers is unmatched anywhere. This practice is a reflection of that understanding.

1. Sit or lie in a comfortable place.

2. Close your eyes and visualize millions of colorful, beautiful, delicate, yet powerful flowers growing inside the bones and through the flesh of your feet.

3. Imagine much larger flowers growing between your toes and springing out of all the joints between your bones. Imagine them penetrating your shins and calves, then your knees, then your thighs and hamstrings, your hip joints and your perineal area. As you move up your body, imagine flowers growing out of each set of joints you encounter, as you become more and more of a living flower being.

4. Using your pelvic bowl as a basin, imagine larger flowers growing up inside you, then

moving out through your anus, your genitals, and your navel. Deep blue-black flowers grow in your coccyx and up through your lumbar vertebrae, escaping outward at the joints between each one. Keep moving up and feel the power and life of the flowers as they bless you and find new ways to grow within you.

5. Imagine brilliant orange flowers growing up through your intestines to your liver, and gold flowers growing in your pancreas, gallbladder, spleen, and diaphragm.

6. Visualize blood-red flowers growing up through your lungs, your breasts, your bronchial tubes.

7. Continue this process up to your thoracic vertebrae, your heart, and your shoulders. Remember to include your veins and arteries, and your blood cells. Imagine flowers growing out through your arms, elbows, forearms, wrists, and hands. Picture long, beautiful flowers growing out of each fingertip into the outside world.

8. Imagine brilliant blue flowers pouring out through your throat, jaw, gums, teeth, mouth, and occiput. Visualize violet flowers growing through and out your ears, your nose, your nostrils, and your sinuses. Up through your brain and all its significant parts—the cerebellum, and the occipital, parietal, temporal, and limbic lobes. Imagine them sprouting in all the white and gray matter in your brain—your medulla, thalamus, and hypothalamus, your corpus collosum and hippocampus, your pituitary and pineal glands, and your brain's four ventricles. Then imagine beautiful purple, lavender, and violet flowers growing out the crown of your head.

9. Now you have become a living flower person, barely resembling your former self. You are literally a new kind of being—beautiful and exotic, able to do things that you were never able to do before.

10. Look around you and notice that the flowers are spreading from your body, out through your feet to the ground and landscape all around you. Flowers are spreading everywhere, enveloping the ground, climbing up trees and into

the clouds, out through the forests and meadows, down into holes in the earth. They are galloping through streets and into homes.

11. Imagine every person, every creature, and every object being delighted, loving the dynamic change, loving the opportunity to become flowers. These flowers race through streams and waterways, lakes and reservoirs; they blanket hills and plains and mountains and valleys and canyons. They push on through swamps, craggy rocks, and badlands. They spread to beaches, lagoons, and oceans, enveloping islands and ships at sea, rushing up onto distant shores and covering everything there—including major cities, highways, buildings, bridges, and anything existing in those places.

12. Imagine flowers moving onward through forests, jungles, tundra, steppes, Arctic and Antarctic ice floes and glaciers, volcanoes—until every speck of the earth's surface is enveloped by them. The planet has become a flower world and still the flowers don't stop.

13. Now imagine the flowers leaping into the atmosphere and making their way to the moon,

then to all the planets—Mars, Venus, Saturn, Jupiter, Mercury, Uranus, and Neptune. See them enveloping Pluto and the other planetoids, and all the moons of all the planets, then moving out to asteroid belts, comets, gas clouds, and every single aspect of the solar system, including the sun.

14. Imagine the sun's rays radiating flowers and flinging them out to other solar systems in the galaxy, until the entire galaxy has been enveloped by them. The celebration is incredible and the gift of flowers spreads at lightning speed, jumping from one galaxy to the next, until the entire physical universe is teeming with flowers of the most incredible sizes, shapes, and colors. The fragrance is overwhelmingly heavenly.

15. Still, the flowers do not stop. In a huge burst of phenomenal power, they leap into the multiverse, to trillions of universes. And all the beings that inhabit them are transformed into flower beings. And the flowers continue on beyond the multiverse, endlessly spreading and transforming everything and nothing.

16. When you have reached the limits of what you can imagine, it is time to head back. On your return voyage, you can witness all of the magnificence of the transformation you have wrought. Travel back through the multiverse, back through our physical universe, back to our own Milky Way galaxy, back to our solar system, back to our planet, back to your land and home, and back to your body.

17. Slowly move your fingers and toes, allowing yourself to become grounded back in ordinary reality.

This practice will inoculate you from negativity, fear, sadness, anger, and other low-vibration frequencies in ways that are difficult to explain. It produces fast results and never fails to make me feel excellent. It can also be performed with others. And you can do shorter or longer versions of it, depending on your needs. It is best, however, to do a longer version periodically.

The Extraordinary
Practice of Falling
into the Arms of Spirit

From our movies to our music to our TV commercials, Western culture is preoccupied with the idea of being in control. This exaltation of control springs directly from a society that prizes productivity, predictability, efficiency, and order. We expect ourselves to perform, produce, and deliver, often on rigid schedules that have nothing to do with the natural rhythms of the planet on which we live. And as if controlling our own behavior weren't hard enough, we often take on the task of controlling the behavior of those around us—which can soon become a full-time occupation! Few want to be controlled—not spouses, not friends, not lovers, not colleagues, not those for whom you are responsible, and certainly not you.

Many people interpret being in control as controlling themselves at all times. But the more you try to control yourself, the more rebellious some aspect of you will become, until you become like a house divided—at war with yourself. You may think that if you are not in control of yourself, you will become crazy—a lunatic, perhaps, or a hopelessly addicted person. Having worked in mental hospitals with the severely mentally ill, however, I can tell you that more mental illness is associated with rigidity and control than with the lack of it. Control is grossly overrated in our culture. And being in control is never associated with tranquility, peacefulness, or happiness.

You may be asking yourself at this point whether you should be in control of your car, or your power tools, or your weight, or your conversations with people to avoid offending them. Yes, you should be. But that is a different kind of control than what I am describing here. That is simply being mindful of what you are doing and how you are doing it. It does not require great effort to control your car or most power tools. In fact, it helps if you are relaxed and not anxious and tight when driving, for example. Rigidity in these situations can be dangerous, because it can make you less responsive than you may need to be. If you try to analyze and control every movement of your muscles, you will be like a dancer trying to "think-dance" instead of just dancing. Thought is not necessary in some situations. You simply need to *know* what you are doing, and thinking and knowing are not the same thing.

Thinking happens in the brain; knowing happens in the heart, in the mind, and all around you. You have to let go and expand to know. But when you think, you constrict, you limit yourself. The processes are very different. Thinking and knowing are worlds apart, but unfortunately, our culture never draws this distinction.

When asked how he managed the Dalai Lama's affairs without thinking, an enlightened Tibetan master replied simply that it was easy. It didn't involve any loss of energy, he said, because knowing was a much more effective way to conduct business and manage life's affairs than the tedium of thinking. Of course, few understood what he was saying.

Shamanic cultures around the world provide a beautiful alternative to control: *surrender*. Rather than attempting to orchestrate every moment of every day, they understand that life unfolds at its own pace and in its own way. Unpredictability is a feature of life on this planet, not a bug in the system. Although many of us dislike surprises and fear uncertainty, shamans understand that surprise and uncertainty are great gifts.

By learning to surrender to the currents of life, we recapture the energy that we waste in attempting to resist it. Moreover, we slowly become aware of the larger forces orchestrating our lives—whether we call it God, Spirit, the Source, or simply the laws of nature. We learn to align ourselves with these powerful forces instead of pushing for our own agendas. Most important, we learn to trust that these forces are already working in our favor. Surrender may feel like a loss of control—and it is—but the more we surrender, the more we learn that losing control can be a very good thing.

Practice: The Art of Surrender

This practice comes from the works of the Persian poet Rumi. However, similar practices have been described by William Blake and by many other enlightened teachers, mystics, and artists. Working with this practice can gradually expand your capacity for surrender, and help you gently release any unhealthy attachment you have to control.

> 1. Lie on your back and imagine yourself falling backward—down, down, down, in a never-ending spiral. This may take some courage, especially if you have a fear of heights or a fear of not being in control.

> 2. At first, practice falling for just a few seconds at a time—whatever you can tolerate without feeling too stressed or activated. Eventually, you

will find that you can just drop or fall backward in your mind's eye and concentrate on the feeling of falling, falling, falling. Believe it or not, this sensation can actually become very refreshing once you've gotten the taste for it.

3. As you fall, keep in mind that you are not going to any specific destination or trying to land in a particular place. You are simply falling. If any intrusive thoughts arise, simply see yourself falling past them, continuing on your downward spiral.

4. As you fall, imagine that you are beginning to fragment into millions of particles of light, letting go of your sense of a solid physical body. Allow this to happen without resistance, and just keep falling. This sensation may be accompanied by streams of light falling away behind you like the trail of a meteor or comet.

5. Eventually, you perceive a pinpoint of very bright light. Let yourself fall toward it, until you are completely surrounded by it. Let yourself be completely enveloped by the loving energy of the divine, or what Rumi referred to as "the Beloved."

6. Realize that by surrendering to the fall, you have arrived at a place of complete love and nourishment.

7. When you feel complete, slowly open your eyes. Wiggle your fingers and toes and take a deep breath to signal that the practice is closed.

The Extraordinary Practice
of Meditating on Death

My mother died at the age of ninety-nine. Sitting by her side on a still December day as she began to transition from this world to the next was one of the most powerful experiences of my life. As she lay in her bed, looking thin and frail yet very peaceful, she described to me how her parents, brothers, and friends were all waiting for her in the next world. She told me that she was looking forward to meeting them, and that she had no further business in this life. "I am finished with everything," she said. "There is nothing more to do." Over the course of several days, she drifted in and out of sleep. As she came nearer to death, she became more and more radiant. "God is so good," she said. "There is so much love in the world."

In the days before death, we enter a liminal space — a misty borderland between this world and the next. In this liminal space, things that may once have seemed important to us — wealth, success, prestige — are quickly forgotten. Instead, we reflect on the people we love, and on our own good and not-so-good deeds. In many cases, the dying suddenly let go of old grudges they've held for years and experience an overall lightening in their demeanor.

Dying to Live

The Toltecs say that one of our greatest follies as humans is to carry the fantasy that our bodies will never die, that they will live forever. Because of this, we put off for tomorrow what we should be taking care of today. We think we have all the time in the world to do what is wise and good. "I'll get around to being kind and generous tomorrow. Right now, I feel like raising hell." "I'll forgive my sister for running off with my boyfriend someday. I'm still really annoyed with her. She's such a bitch." "I'll have that conversation with my dad, and apologize to him later for wrecking his car. I still think it's funny. He deserved it anyway, the ass."

But sometimes "later" and "tomorrow" never come. I was once unkind to a girl I dated in high school and blamed her for something that was not her fault. Several years later, her cousin told me she had died suddenly of a brain tumor. I felt terrible, knowing that it was too late to set things right.

During life, we witness many deaths and are involved with death in many ways. Our pets die, our relatives die, and sometimes friends die unexpectedly. There is just no avoiding it. Over the many years I have been a psychotherapist, I have lost a number of clients to death, some of whom I had worked with for years. Illness, accidents, age, suicide, accidental overdoses— these are all ways that people leave our lives, some with no warning. I have had the good fortune to lead memorial services for some of my students who have passed over, and on a variety of occasions, I have assisted others during their dying process, and this has been a wonderful opportunity to learn. Yet we still convince ourselves that, somehow, death won't happen to us, so we put things off.

Shamanic cultures developed useful spiritual practices that remind us that death is a part of living, and never far away. The Wixarika believe that our death follows us around, watching us over our left shoulders; then, when it is time for us to pass over, it grabs us. Therefore it is best, they say, to keep death in an advisory role as long as it is accompanying us. I like this idea because it is so practical.

Meditating on death is such a powerful experience that I have included three practices based on this idea. Use them to make peace with death as it exists in your day-to-day life, and to prepare yourself for the bigger transition into the next world.

Practice: Meeting Death as an Ally

This is one of my favorite practices for keeping death near in an advisory capacity. This is most useful when you are experiencing the death of someone you know, or when you know that death has come for you.

1. Sit in a comfortable position where you have some privacy and call upon the spirit of death to visit with you.

2. Turn and look over your left shoulder. Visualize the spirit of death there and invite it to come over and talk with you. This spirit may look like the classic grim reaper with a hood and scythe, but there is no reason for death to look so creepy or scary. Actually, the job of the spirit of death is to assist you when your own death draws nigh. You can see it as an angelic form or just as a kind and friendly teacher who wants to help you pass over—a midwife, so to speak, when the time comes. For some, the spirit of death may show up as an animal or in some other form.

3. Say hello to the spirit and thank it for its service to you and to all who pass over to the other side. Ask it any questions you may have about

the process of death, what you can do to prepare better for it, or what kind of a death would suit you.

4. Listen carefully to the answers you imagine you hear. Share any concerns you have with the spirit, any fears you have been carrying about how death feels, or any fears you may have of not knowing when death will come. Perhaps you are afraid it will be painful, or that it will take you by surprise in a horrible way. Share these concerns and listen to what your advisor has to say to help you.

5. When you feel complete, thank the spirit for being accessible and answering your questions.

You may want to perform this practice at different times, because at different points in your life you may have different feelings and concerns about death and this will help you get used to the idea that, indeed, your time will come.

Practice: Mongolian Death Practice

This is a classic shamanic death practice that, if approached with curiosity, can be quite fun. It can be performed as a group in a large space or solo. If you perform it alone, you will need a space with good clearance all around you, about ten feet in every direction—perhaps outside in a meadow or a clearing. If you are performing it in a group, keep the participants about ten feet apart.

1. Begin by slowly spinning counterclockwise with your eyes almost closed—open just enough to avoid bumping into someone or something. Don't spin too slowly, but don't go too fast either. Keep spinning until you grow tired, or until you lose your balance and fall to the ground. Be careful not to hit your head. This falling represents a kind of symbolic death. Some people fall right away and some take more time. Don't try to resist falling; just let it happen naturally.

2. As you lie there, imagine that you are in the center of a circle of skulls that are all facing you.

3. Imagine that a hot wind begins to blow. Your lifeless body is being tousled by this wind and is being dried out by it. Your skin shrivels and begins to shred. Pieces are blowing away in the wind, revealing raw flesh that then begins to dry out and shred as well. Your hair falls out

in chunks and blows away, leaving your skull bare. Your nose, lips, ears, and eyes decay and dry out and fall away. Your bones are beginning to show—your skull and the bones of your feet and hands and elbows and knees. Everything is drying out and shredding, and chunks are blowing away in the increasingly wild wind that blows hot sand like a sandblaster all over what is left of you. White bones are revealed everywhere and your organs tumble out, reduced to leather by the heat and dust. Eventually, there is no flesh or meat left, just brittle bones that fall apart into chips and then blow away. Only the largest bones remain, and they are quickly disappearing in the raging wind.

4. There is nothing left of your body at all, and yet you are still aware and conscious without it and this is curious.

5. Imagine that you begin to build a brand-new body out of fresh ingredients from the fertile earth. The wind and heat are gone; the temperature is comfortable. There is a rich moisture in the air.

6. Slowly, as if by a hidden process, calcium is drawn up from the earth and forms the bones of your skeleton.

7. Damp soil full of minerals and plants and wood come together to create fresh and new organs that are covered by tendons and muscle, and then by skin. There is rich red blood running in new arteries and veins. Your heart is beating and your eyes and ears are forming and functioning. Your hair is growing and flowing in all the right places. Your genitals appear.

8. This is your new body. Occupy it and feel its rich textures and life force mobilizing it with vitality and flexibility.

9. Wiggle your new toes and fingers, move your new limbs, and enjoy. Rise to your feet and greet the earth with your new body.

Practice: Dying to Something

When I was an undergraduate, a philosophy professor showed our class a film of Krishnamurti, a Hindu philosopher of great renown, who was delivering a lecture on getting to know death. He said that the best way to familiarize yourself with death while you were still living was to select something and choose to "die to it." By doing this, you would really discover what death meant.

I was quite impressed by this teaching and could grasp the value of it, so I decided to accept his challenge and choose something from my own life to die to. The idea was that even though whatever I chose would be available to everyone else and remain in the physical world, I was making the choice that it would no longer be available to me—ever in this lifetime. According to Krishnamurti, this could be an object, a habit, a person, or even a way of seeing things. Many *sadhus* in India raise an arm up and leave it raised for life as a way of learning the same thing. I considered this practice to be self-maiming, however, and I didn't believe in that, so I decided to choose an object instead. At that time I was a coffee drinker, and although I loved the taste and ritual of it, I did not like how the caffeine in it made me feel— uncomfortably jittery and shaky. So I decided never to drink another cup of coffee in this lifetime. The idea scared me because it felt so final, so much like a death. What if I changed my mind? The challenge was that I could not go back on my choice, because I had died to it.

This one exercise taught me more about death than I imagined possible. To this day, I have never drunk another cup of coffee. I live with a wife who loves coffee and drinks it every day, as do my children. I have traveled in Turkey and places where everyone drinks their sacred coffee multiple times a day. Coffee franchises appear to have taken over the world, but still no coffee. I died to it that day. It is not in my world, and never will be. It has been about fifty-six years since I died to coffee. And I have never once regretted it.

Here are the steps of the practice:

1. Carefully consider what you will die to.

2. Then die to it.

That's it. There's nothing else to it. Just take a minute or so to make your choice. *Then do it.* But don't be fooled. Although this practice may seem overly simple and very brief, it is overwhelmingly powerful—a truly great shamanic practice. What will you choose?

PART SIX

Perceptual Practices

In my experience, 99 percent of spiritual practice comes down to learning to see the world in a new way—to see beauty instead of ugliness, possibility instead of limitations, abundance instead of scarcity, and friends instead of competitors. In the immortal words of William Blake: "If the doors of perception were cleansed, everything would appear to man as it is—infinite. For man has closed himself up, till he sees all things thro' narrow chinks in his cavern." The practices in this section all have the goal of widening those "narrow chinks" through which we've become accustomed to viewing the world, allowing us to see the true beauty and divinity in every moment.

The act of perceiving means noticing what was not noticed before. The act of perceiving actually alchemically transforms reality. It creates a new world. All the practices in this section quite literally transform reality, not just simply shifting our focus, but actively creating—just as we humans were meant to do.

The Extraordinary
Practice of Discovering
You Are No-Thing

I first got in touch with this notion of being "no-thing" by working with my physical body. All my life I have been an athlete, very aware of my body and how I could get it to perform at my limit. The first sport I played was baseball. Then, when I was in high school, I ran cross-country and middle distances in track—the half mile and the mile. I was so committed to running and loved it so much that I used to wake up at 5:30 in the morning and ride my motorcycle down to where the Los Angeles Track Club worked out. At that time, they had sub-four-minute milers working out under a Hungarian Olympic coach and that was a big deal. I managed to get him to give me some workouts, which I followed, and I improved enormously. Later, I learned to ski, to climb mountains and raft rivers; I do some martial arts and practice yoga and Qi Gong. Of course,

I picked up some injuries along the way. My body was me and I was my body, and so I was also all the pain and hardship I put it through.

Little did I know that the body is not what I thought it was. When I first began training and doing all these sports, I took the conventional point of view that my consciousness was wrapped up in my experience of my body, and that I was more or less in my body in the same way that I was in my car. My body even has a name tag and I answer to it. But little by little, as I did the practices in this book and studied spiritual traditions and philosophies over many years, that convention began to break down.

I can't say exactly how it happened, but somehow, someway, I began to recognize that I am *not* my body. After a time, I realized that my body did not exist in the way I thought it did. In fact, this body that I appeared to have was just a convenience, a useful hallucination of a fleshy vehicle to allow Spirit to experience physicality.

This does not discount the body or make it somehow obsolete. The body has its own reality from its own point of view. It is an amazing miracle in its makeup and abilities. I am so grateful to have access to this body—a most useful tool—and to use it for its true purpose. In fact, I like it more than ever before. It is a very faithful hallucination, somewhat like a shadow that appears everywhere I go. So I still do my practices every day, but now with greater understanding, because I know my body's true nature.

I have come to realize that my experience of my body comes through a number of avenues—sensations, feelings, perceptions, pressures, and images that are all provided through its sense organs. Waves of light at different vibrational frequencies and amplitudes are recorded by the senses, then transferred to the brain via nerves that collate and interpret this information into my culturally defined impression of a physical body. At no time do I have any direct experience of my *whole* body. What I know of my body is a constantly changing interpretation of the information that my senses are transferring.

At any time, these impressions could be interpreted in a different way through techniques like hypnosis or altered perceptions. Thus, the knowledge of my body is not stable or consistent. All the sensations that it is moving or going somewhere are provided by my sense organs. I never have any direct evidence that my body has gone anywhere. So much for all that running. On the other hand, my consciousness is stable and consistent and never goes anywhere. It is the same as when I was a small child. Consciousness is just the phenomena of being aware of whatever seems to be happening and, in addition, it is always aware of itself.

The narrative that goes with the body and its name is similarly ephemeral and subject to many changes of interpretation. There is no direct evidence that I was actually here ten minutes ago, one year ago, or ten years ago. My memories of what happened in my life could have been implanted five seconds ago, giving me an apparent history. This is all consistent with a Buddhist understanding that behind every apparently physical object there is only emptiness. There is no one here to have anything happen *to*. All there actually is that is undeniable is awareness—or consciousness or presence, if you will—and that awareness is not personal, but infinite. And yes, it is always in the eternally present moment. This presence is also not a physical object that is subject to any boundaries, edges, or limits. The guy named José is just a convenient fiction so Spirit (also not a physical object) can have another unique experience of itself.

Don't look too closely or you will find that this book is not actually real either. It is another convenient fiction to help remind you of what you really are before you forgot and thought you were an object. Some may find these words frightening or disagreeable. Who wants to think of themselves as nothing? But let's write that word differently. Who wants to think of themselves as *no-thing*? That's better, isn't it? We are not objects or things. We are instead incredible beings of

light and pure potential who are not confined to physicality. To be purely physical would be to be in prison,
and we are not prisoners unless we think we are. And
if we think that, the game is over. That old paradigm is
pure hell. Yet, unfortunately, that is what most people
think of themselves.

We are leaving that old paradigm and entering a
new one—the one I have been describing here. Better
get used to it, because, eventually, everyone will understand that they are no-thing and be able to function
more or less out of this understanding. That will spell
the end of war and include many other beneficial results
that right now seem impossible even to imagine. The
paradigm of limitation is disappearing.

When we are stuck in the old paradigm that has
brought this imagined world so much misery and suffering, we are restricted to thinking—thinking, analyzing, and using only reason. This is quite restrictive
and keeps us in the dualistic world of separate objects.
When we slowly let go of our constant thinking or
monkey mind, we have moments of silence, moments
of freedom, moments of expansion. This is nothing to
fear. It does not indicate annihilation or extinction. It
means freedom to begin to *know*. Remember—thinking
and knowing are not the same thing. Knowing is freedom; thinking is mostly restrictive. The challenge is to
keep don't know mind.

Fortunately, there have been pathfinders before us who have made these same discoveries, and some were written down by their disciples. Jesus, Siddhartha Gautama, Lao Tsu, Krishna, Isis, Bridget, Quan Yin, and so many others about whom we don't know have trod this ground before us and slowly begun to understand and know. And whenever the truth is known by anyone and expressed, it explodes into reality and changes everything.

We are approaching a time when all will realize a measure of this truth, each according to their own potential. All the cells of the larger body of humanity are waking up and exploding with light. When the great teacher Jesus referred to the second coming, he was not referring to himself, but rather to this understanding and knowing that awareness and consciousness would explosively expand. When we acknowledge and understand this, we realize that we have to take responsibility for our own bodies and make sure that their cells will also be ready to explode with light and the supreme intelligence of the universe.

Yet, although our bodies are no-things, they are our vehicles in this imagined virtual-reality world and they need attention to support their potential. The practice below can help you regain your integrity, your power, your love, your light, and your right to be present at this moment in time. From this point of view, our bodies are miraculous songs, incredible happenings, beautiful suchness. Carlos Castaneda spoke these truths in his descriptions of his experiences with Don Juan, although they can sometimes be hard to ferret out amid all the drama of his stories.

In reality, however, the clues and signs are everywhere if you just look. One of things I love about shamanism is its regular references to these truths. Shamans understand that life is a dream that can be molded by our intention. They believe that with our intention, we can move mountains. But, in truth, the intention is not ours. It is Spirit's intention working through us that makes the impossible possible, that controls storm clouds, and literally moves what appear to be objects like mountains.

Practice: Becoming No-Thing

When Steve Jobs died, his last words were: "Oh wow. Oh wow. Oh wow." When movie critic Roger Ebert was dying, he said wonderingly to his wife: "It's all a hoax." What people say on their deathbeds is worth noting. You can learn a lot from observations like these. They are clues to what is true. This practice can help you to discover some of these clues for yourself.

1. Sit comfortably, relax, and breathe evenly and deeply for a couple minutes.

2. Ask yourself these questions: "Who am I? What am I? What is my body?" Give yourself some time to contemplate these questions and give some answers.

3. Now ask yourself: "How do I know I am here?" Notice the reaction in your body—its sensations, feelings, and emotions; its perceptions, memories, and reflections. Stay with these responses.

4. Ask yourself: "How do I know I am having this feeling? This sensation? This idea?" Dig down deep and do not be satisfied with superficial answers.

5. See that you are a collection of many different variables, sensations, and perceptions. What have you been taught to believe about your body? Question, question, question. Have you ever seen your face directly, not in a mirror? You can touch it, but those are just more sensations being recorded in your brain. Where is the actual proof that you are here and that you are not just making it all up?

6. Examine your memories of yourself being here. Are any of these memories actual proof that you weren't created one second ago along with your so-called memories? How do you know you are not just some very good actor playing you?

7. What is really animating your body? What is its source of aliveness and presence?

8. Above all, don't be satisfied with any of your answers. They are all suspect, designed to make you *not* question.

Have periodic sessions like this. Keep at it. Let the world as you know it fall apart. It won't hurt you. In fact, it will be the best thing that ever happened to you. What is right around the corner from no-thing is *everything*. But you have to be no-thing before you can be everything.

The Extraordinary
Practice of Seeing
the Divine in Everything

There are infinite possibilities in the universe. One of those possibilities is what we call the physical plane—the plane of materiality occupied by human beings, animals, plants, minerals, stars, planets, moons, etc. The consciousness of Spirit is always extending itself, finding new modes of expression, and this is true throughout all the possibilities of the universe.

Many religions have taught that the physical plane is a place of very low vibration, a place of sin and misery. The only salvation, they say, is to avoid it altogether and concentrate on getting back to heaven or the "higher" planes of existence. On the surface, this almost seems as if it could be true, but it is not. God Consciousness is pervasive throughout all the planes, all the possibilities, and is ever present in the physical plane through every particle, every vibration, every aspect. There is no place where God Consciousness is not. This is a simple truth, but people tend to have a very difficult time understanding it.

What if I see a dog turd on the sidewalk? Is God Conscious in that? Of course. There is no place where it is not. Well, what about in the toilet? Is it there as well? Of course. There is no place where it is not. What about in the dumpster or in a serial killer? Yes, of course. There is no place where it is not. This can be very upsetting to some, but that is just the way it is. Can you make an exception and say that God Consciousness is everywhere else, but not in your dirty socks? No, how could that be possible? The very definition of God, the Great Spirit, is that God is the creator of all that is. There is nothing outside of God Consciousness. If there were even one exception, God would not be the creator of all that is. Pretty simple, really. What is there not to understand?

And yet, every day, most people decide for themselves what does and does not have God Consciousness. Those filthy people over there? Nope, not God. That dead baby? Nope, not God. That battlefield? No, definitely not God. That slime-bag politician? Nope, not God. Those people having lusty sex? Not God. That heroin addict passed out over there or that doctor performing an abortion? That black widow spider? That drug dealer? Those immigrants? Those perverts? No, not God. Well, that is an awful lot of "not God," considering that God Consciousness is by definition everywhere, in everything.

When people decide that something is not of Spirit, they open the door to the possibility that they themselves may not be of God, or that they could do something that could cast them out of where God is. But this introduces a massive problem—the problem of damnation, the problem of hell, the problem of an inferno filled with horrible suffering. When people do this, they end up damning themselves—and everything and everyone else. Why would anyone want to do that? In fact, the only conclusion we can come to about these self-created nasty fears of doom is that they are based on something that is fundamentally impossible—that there can be any space or object or person that is not God.

Human beings and other individually ensouled species throughout the physical universe are highly evolved concentrations of God Consciousness that are self-aware and aware of their surroundings. Moreover, they are capable of being aware of their origins or source. Not all of them exhibit this awareness consciously, because they are still evolving, still waking up from a state of ignorance in which they are capable of low-vibrational attitudes, beliefs, and behaviors. Nevertheless, they are highly concentrated conscious beings who, through their perceptions and ability to focus, have a strong influence and impact on their own reality.

How they see themselves and their surroundings actually temporarily *creates* who they are and what their surroundings are like. All human beings are involved in the agreed upon reality at any given time, even though they may decry it or condemn it. But this only reinforces consensual reality, because that is how resistance works. What we resist persists.

Because our consciousness is new by the universe's standards, it is somewhat immature and allows us to produce ugliness and destructiveness in our surroundings. We could easily misinterpret this to mean that the physical plane is inherently miserable and evil, a place of suffering. But it is only a place of suffering if we see it that way. Imagine that you pick up a diamond in the rough and it appears as just another ugly stone. That is what you see and that is what you believe. The diamond is there in all its beauty, but you don't believe it unless someone with experience tells you to scrape off the surface to reveal the precious gemstone beneath. When you do, beauty appears where only ugliness appeared before.

The way to change reality is simply to see it differently. But you have to do that without engaging in denial and delusion. To see reality differently, you must recognize that you are participating in cocreation. You must agree with those around you that whatever you see and experience you have had a hand in creating. Moreover, you must be open to cocreating another possibility and be able to accept how that possibility appears without judgment and with neutrality. And most important, you must recognize that every possibility is permeated with and expressed through the higher vibration of the divine. Despite its apparent ugliness, you must be willing to see it with love in your heart.

This is the alchemical process that transforms the physical plane to a higher octave where beauty trumps ugliness and suffering. This process restores the physical plane to what it is capable of being—a mirror of Spirit. The truth then sets you and it free—sets everyone free. This is the primary purpose of being a human being. Somehow we just forgot our purpose, and got distracted for a long time with other activities that, while engrossing, are much less gratifying in the long run. Nonetheless, the diamond is still there and it is genuine. It is ultimately what everything will be transformed into.

It takes enormous courage and faith to see things in this way. And when we do, we risk appearing to others as if we are mad. But when enough concentrated consciousness acts together, the physical plane will be utterly transformed. Until then, it will be transformed in bits and pieces, in very localized ways, through the eyes of individuals. And little by little, the garden is revealed.

With this in mind, what should you do when you see something that appears to be ugly? Let go of anger; let go of depression; let go of sadness. See it with love. See it as the divine. See it for what is actually there. This goes for everything in life. See homeless people, war zones, crime scenes, and political horrors with love. See drug deals, corporate malfeasance, poverty, and racism as aspects of the divine. See hunger, mistreated immigrants, polluted water, and littered beaches as beautiful. Does this mean that you do nothing about these situations—just smugly look at them differently? No. You create miracles by taking small actions that accompany your new way of perceiving. You recognize yourself as highly concentrated awareness that is empowered to transform reality at will.

We humans really are specially empowered, but only if we recognize that we are. Otherwise, we operate from a cancerous ignorance. In order to step into our power, we have to take responsibility for what we are capable of being and doing. We are not helpless victims; we are not doomed to suffering. We are extensions and expressions of Spirit. Until we recognize this, we are relegated to the worst the physical plane has to offer. Doesn't seem like much of a choice, does it?

Christian mystic Meister Eckhart wrote: "The eye through which I see God is the eye through which God sees me." In other words, our ability to know and comprehend the divine is bidirectional. The more we see God, the more God sees us. The more we keep an eye out for the divine, the more divinity is revealed to us. It is the quality of our perception that activates the divine all around us.

Practice: Awakening God Consciousness

This practice provides you with a simple tool for awakening your own ability to see God, and letting God see you. It could not be simpler, and you can do it almost anytime, almost anywhere. Do it often and keep it short.

1. Go to your trash can, preferably when it is full and nasty with fish bones, rotting bananas, scrapings from various meals, fur from the cat or dog, and items like vacuum cleaner bags.

2. Open the lid and look carefully. Inspect everything. Is there anything outside of God Consciousness in there? Breathe in the aroma.

3. Look at the most disgusting thing you can find and contemplate that God Consciousness is in there permeating it. See that it is just so! See that this is exactly how it was meant to be at this moment—a perfect piece of trash. See and

feel the suchness of it. Can you accept its presence along with everything else? It has its place in the universe. There is divinity here, something sacred.

4. As a variation on this practice, go for a walk in a run-down area and notice the cigarette butts, the candy wrappers, the beer cans, the discarded needles, the broken bits of glass littering the landscape. Can you accept them as having divinity within them?

5. Look around. What else can you find? A mongrel dog with fleas? A person muttering to no one at all? A broken-down vehicle gathering dust and leaves? Graffiti on a wall? Loud, thumping music coming from a car? Sirens? You get the idea. Can you see these things as perfect? As full of God Consciousness? Can you unlock their holiness with your awareness?

6. Turn on the TV and watch a few minutes of a news program or a channel that is wildly out of step with your own values or politics. Allow your habitual feelings of disgust or outrage to subside. Can you sense that somewhere within these folks there is a diamond? Beauty and

divinity? God Consciousness? Can you feel love for them, even as you disagree?

7. Understand that as you witness all these things in a neutral way, you are taking the first step toward changing reality. The second step is seeing them as divine.

The Extraordinary
Practice of Raising the
Vibration of Everything

Human beings occupying the physical plane mostly vibrate within the range of one major octave; they may move up and down the scale, but they confine themselves to this one octave. At its lowest vibrations, the octave resonates with fear and those things that go with fear, like feeling victimized, martyred, helpless, or powerless. At its highest vibrations, it resonates with fondness, love of family and friends, general satisfaction, and happiness. In between, there are all the familiar states we witness in ourselves and others at various times, ranging upward from aggression, judging, blaming, jealousy, and envy, to sorrow and grief, to play, fun, and excitement, to inspiration, creativity, and enthusiasm, and finally to generosity, kindness, forgiveness, calm, and peacefulness.

These feelings and states are all available to human beings in the general course of living. Each of them is a field or vibration that can be discerned and experienced. Up and down the scale we go. Some people are stuck most of the time in one or another of the lower frequencies, and some choose to rise up and spend more of their time in the higher ones. All these vibrations provide learning of one sort or another. Yet hardly any of these vibrations are truly expansive, because they are strongly tied to expectations, thoughts, feelings, and external conditions to which we react. From these states, it is very difficult to impact or influence the environment in a way that doesn't end up in some kind of suffering, because they are temporary or impermanent conditions.

Almost all of these states are intimately tied to the thinking process that tends to analyze, define, and label everything experienced, and this leads to a shrinking of awareness. In these states, we tend to divide our experience into fragments that we can further analyze, and this leads to even more myopic views of reality. Ultimately, this results in "specialization." We have specialists in every field who have mastered the operations of very small units of awareness, but in so doing have lost the big picture, the intricate web of connection with everything. This, for example, is the current state of medical science and it is what limits its effectiveness. Everyone knows a lot about a little bit. It is very difficult to rise in vibration when starting from this state of affairs. Everything in our perception is just too fragmented. And if we cannot raise our own vibration, then it is almost impossible for us to raise the vibration of our environment or situation.

But it is possible to let go of our persistent myopic analysis and engage in more unified states of awareness like gratitude, love, awe, forgiveness, kindness, and compassion. These states, rather than narrowing our focus, are expansive and large in context; they move upward and outward. They are part of a higher octave that we can reach when we know how.

The ego, or little self, does not like these higher-octave perceptions, because they threaten its agenda of keeping the personality distracted and afraid, the better to dominate it. These higher vibrational states tend to unify rather than critique, judge, separate, define, label, and diagnose. Notice that these higher states lead to greater relaxation or a letting go, while the myopic states require and wish for more control. You have to surrender more to forgive or be kind than you do when you are diagnosing or engaging in critical thinking.

These thinking activities lead to a feeling of *being* right, while forgiveness or kindness lead to a deep sense of *knowing* what is right. These are two very different states. One is controlled by the ego; one is fielded by essence. From states of love, gratitude, or awe, for example, there is no speculation, just very simple, very direct knowing. Thinking leads to limited types of knowledge, but kindness, for example, often comes with a "don't know mind": "I don't know why, but I am motivated to be kind in this situation." "This dog just tried to bite me. I don't know why, but I am going to try to clean his wound anyway." "I don't know why, but I am finding myself going out of my way to take this stranger to the airport. I am just aware that it feels right and good."

When we operate from these octaves, we can awaken the higher vibrational states that are available but that may not be obvious because they have been slumbering under a layer of neglect. In truth, everything already has higher vibrational dimensions — trees, fields, people, animals, plants, and even man-made objects. But the way we perceive and treat them may be hiding their higher vibrational aspects, making them appear dreary, dull, or lacking in light. Seeing them as full of light makes them light up from within to reveal their truth. This can be the case with people too, but we can't make them be filled with light unless they agree to it, because they have free will. Sometimes people embrace darkness because they are learning a tough lesson. Some embrace it because it allows them to feel sorry for themselves or gives them something to complain about righteously. We just don't always know the reason, and in many ways it does not matter. What matters is that we respect others' choices to remain in darkness a while longer, knowing that they will emerge sooner or later when they choose to.

So we raise the vibration of what we can when we can, but only after we have raised our own vibration to its natural state by focusing on what is inspiring: on things and people we love, on things for which we are grateful, and on acts of kindness and compassion. We offer the higher vibration to our brothers and sisters, and then leave it up to them whether they will accept it or not.

Practice: Rising up the Scale

This powerful and impactful practice is similar to the practice of seeing the divine in everything, but with some additional perspectives. It can help you to see random people as expressions of their multidimensional selves, occupying many time frames, locations, states of consciousness, and dimensions all at once.

Go to a public place and observe the people you find there. Don't judge them; just observe. Then consider that the homeless person you see shuffling along may at this very moment be an enlightened Tibetan Buddhist master in another lifetime and an axe murderer in yet another. Consider that the poverty-stricken mother of ten you see may be an opera singer of great accomplishment and acclaim in another dimension. These are all expressions of her eternally present multidimensional self, which is already divine, holy, sacred, blessed, and completely enlightened. You can see her in her parts and judge her, throwing her under the bus, or you can see her in her wholeness and bless her. And, no matter what, her essence will register that and glow with light.

Consider that the drug addict you encounter may be the one who saves you in a distant lifetime, or may be the love of your life in another dimension. You don't know. There are only two possibilities for our egoic little selves. We either don't know anything, or we know what we need to know. But our multidimensional selves know everything there is to know. Thus, there is no problem for them to think through and figure out. There is nothing to fix, nothing to do here but just be aware.

The Extraordinary Practice of Being Aware, Conscious, and Present

We humans are like bowls that are filled with content. Think of that bowl as context. The bowl remains stable and consistent, but the contents are constantly changing and impermanent. The context is our awareness, our consciousness, and our presence, which is stable and consistent. Our content is our narrative, the various incidents of our lives, which are unstable and impermanent. And that leads us to a natural question: Which one are we—the context or the content?

All the great spiritual teachers say the same thing. We are the context, the space in which everything happens. The content cannot be us because it appears and vanishes constantly. So the person who carries our name and our history is fictional and to some degree unimportant. This is the key to the end of suffering, and that is certainly an attractive possibility.

Empty space, however, is not the be-all and end-all of our existence. If that were all there is, existence would be rather dull. But empty space can actually be self-luminous, like the sun, and that luminosity can be described as the supreme intelligence of the universe. This intelligence streaming through empty space is what Eckhart Tolle describes as "transcendent spaciousness." And it is this spaciousness that constitutes our awareness, which is indescribably blissful. The following practice can help you "feel into" this transcendent spaciousness to arrive at full awareness.

Practice: Expanding into Awareness

Begin by suddenly stopping whatever you are doing and asking yourself any of the following questions: "Am I alive?" "Am I present?" "Am I aware?" "Am I conscious?" "Am I being?" The answer should be obvious right away. The answer to all these questions is "yes."

Sink into this awareness. Feel yourself falling into it. Feel how it expands in all directions, urging you to be bigger and bigger and more expansive. It may extend far beyond your body. You may even lose track of the momentary sensations of your body as you expand your awareness to the cosmos or even just to your region.

Practice being big. It's okay. You can be as big as the cosmos if you wish. This is what human beings are actually designed for—being expansive. Think of people who have displayed this kind of greatness, this expansiveness, in their lives—people like Gandhi, Pema Chödrön, Leonardo da Vinci, Jesus, Mary Magdalene, Siddhartha Gautama, Mother Teresa, Quan Yin, Thich Nhat Hanh, Amma, Zoroaster, Marie Curie, Cleopatra, and Abraham Lincoln.

As you practice, you will get better at maintaining this awareness while you are engaged in other activities—perhaps singing, writing, reading, walking, or talking to someone. It may seem difficult at first, or even a little strange, but it will gradually become easier and yield amazing and interesting results that you can only experience through practice.

The Extraordinary Practice
of Tracking False Gods

When I was a child, I remember being both impressed and terrified by the biblical commandment: "I am the Lord thy God; thou shalt not have false gods before me." To me, this sounded like the command of an all-powerful God who would dole out dire punishment if disobeyed. I imagined this angry God sending down lightning bolts and condemning people to hellfire forever. As I matured, these images gradually faded, but, now and then, the threatening commandment would come into my mind, and I would contemplate its meaning.

Later in life, I came to understand this commandment not as a threat, but as a loving reminder to return constantly to my higher self. It enjoined me not to get distracted by the "false gods" of worry, hypervigilance, or constant mental chatter. Spirit—expressed as my higher self, with its wisdom, care, and unconditional love—is "the lord my God," and I'm happier when I don't place other false gods before it. In contrast, when

I let myself become distracted by false gods or even worship them, I find myself living from my frightened lower self and I become miserable!

False gods can take many forms. Over the course of your life, you may have many different false gods, discarding one set of them as you grow in wisdom and self-realization, only to replace them with a slightly subtler or more devious set. For example, when you are in your twenties, you may chase the gods of sex, fame, and fortune, believing that these will make you important. By the time you reach your thirties, you may have recognized the emptiness of these external goals—but now you may strive to be the perfect parent, partner, or employee, and feel worried and afraid when you fall short of these goals. Or you may feel threatened by others with whom you feel competitive and worry that they will fare better than you in business and life.

False gods can be highly destructive, or they can be relatively benign, but what they all have in common is that they distract us from the unconditional love that is at the heart of all of existence. They are not external golden calves, but rather internal parasites within our very own minds that need to be flushed out.

You can tell that you've fallen under the sway of a false god when you find yourself obsessing over something—money, or social status, or achievements in your career. If you find yourself worrying about how you are going to get something, or how you are going to avoid something, you know there's a false god lurking nearby.

Identifying false gods and noticing how they operate is a form of stalking or tracking that shamans use to eradicate energy leaks in their lives. For lions and other predators, stalking prey is a very important part of the hunt. It may take them many days to track their prey, but it takes them only a few seconds to bring it down if their stalking was done carefully and thoroughly. Ask yourself: "Am I a predator or prey?" The truth is that you are a predator whether you know it or not, and whether you like it or not. Learn to use your predatory nature in a good way by tracking your own false gods. By tracking them down, you weaken them and strengthen yourself. The Egyptians understood this and exemplified it in the goddess Set, who oversaw the war we wage with ourselves in our efforts to become free.

Practice: Destroying False Gods

This practice will help you identify the false gods that are operating in your life, so that you can return to the true god of your higher self and enjoy its many gifts. Its goal is as much to destroy false gods as it is to make you aware of them.

1. In a notebook, make a list of all the things you fear, all the things about which you worry

or obsess. This can be more effective if you list these things over several days. These may include unlikely events like dying in a plane crash, or everyday things like wondering what a certain person really thinks of you. Be thorough. You may be surprised at how long this list becomes.

2. Go through your list and see if you can identify any recurring themes. How many of your fears or worries have to do with money? How many have to do with other people's judgments and opinions? How many have to do with vanity, ego, or pride? Each of these is a false god.

3. Ask yourself who you would be without this fear, without these energy leaks, these obsessions and addictions. Imagine this state of being in detail. If you weren't afraid of failure, rejection, discomfort, or pain, what would that feel like? If you were not distracted by these worries, how would you feel? Call these more positive feelings into your body and mind.

4. Consider that this feeling of security, inner peace, expansion, and unconditional love is the true God, expressed through your higher self,

your awareness, and your presence, which are always with you.

5. The next time you realize you've been triggered by a false god, gently say the words: "False god!" Then reorient to your higher self.

The Extraordinary Practice of Taking Responsibility

If there's one piece of advice that my shamanic students resist the most it's when I suggest that they start taking 100 percent responsibility for their lives—both the good parts *and* the difficult parts. Human beings have a well-documented tendency to take credit for the positive events and outcomes in their lives, while ascribing negative outcomes to uncontrollable outside forces. Most people feel that they have no responsibility for all the events of the world in which they are not directly involved—for example, war, poverty, crime, hunger, homelessness, and corporate greed. "After all, that is all happening 'over there,' and I can't do anything about it."

If you want to make rapid progress on your spiritual path, however, it helps to challenge these biases on a regular basis. One effective way of doing this is to take responsibility for *everything* that happens in your life—even, or perhaps especially, those things that are completely out of your control. Now just to be clear,

I don't mean blaming yourself for everything that happens to you or feeling guilty or at fault for the random events of life. What I mean by taking responsibility is learning to see more and more of life as being part of you, not separate from you. In all truth, it is not your ego that can ever take responsibility for the world; it is your essence self.

This is a true power position, acknowledged by sages and spiritual masters throughout history. It means that, in order to be truly response-able, you need to be identified with your higher self, not your ego. Your higher self is, by nature, never separate from anything. By identifying with it, you start to break down those illusory boundaries between you and not-you. After all, where do "you" really end? At the end of your hair and the tips of your fingers? At the boundary where your breath is detectable, or your scent? At the distance at which your voice carries? How do you know that the entire world, or indeed the universe, is not part of "you"? All enlightened masters discover the truth of this.

Being responsible for your life means responding to your life in all its vastness—with love, wisdom, and an open mind.

Practice: Accepting the Vastness of Life

This practice teaches you to expand your concept of responsibility and, with it, your concept of yourself.

1. Sit in a posture of meditation that feels comfortable for you.

2. Take a few deep breaths and ground yourself.

3. Starting with your body and moving outward, begin to name the things for which you are responsible, or to which you are able to respond. For example:

- I am responsible for my teeth, my hair, and my breath.

- I am responsible for my anger, my sadness, and my frustration.

- I am responsible for my work, my relationships, and my home.

- I am responsible for the rocks, the rivers, and the springs.

- I am responsible for the sun, the moon, and the earth.

4. After saying or thinking each phrase, allow yourself to imagine that all of the things you have listed are under your tender, wise, and loving care. Extend benevolence to all of the things you have listed.

5. Now let's up the ante:

- I am responsible for all I see, sense, and feel.

- I am responsible for all that I experience.

- I am responsible for all that I can imagine.

- I am responsible for all that I am aware of.

- I am responsible for everything I hear of or know about.

- I am responsible for all conditions in the world.

- I am responsible for everything I am unaware of, but that are part of the human experience.

- I am responsible for how I see things, how I feel about things, what I don't want to see.

6. Notice how asserting responsibility for ever-larger parts of the universe makes you feel. What is it like to feel responsible for trees, planets, and other things you've probably been taught aren't really part of you? What is the true boundary between you and not-you, if such a boundary exists at all? Does asserting responsibility for the whole universe make the universe feel friendlier? Does it make you feel more capable? Does it give you a sense of your true multidimensional self?

The Extraordinary Practice
of Making Offerings

On my visits to Peru, I've had the honor of witnessing many traditional despacho ceremonies conducted by the shamans there. The Spanish word *despacho* means "to send," and a despacho ceremony is a way of offering gratitude to the Earth Mother for the many gifts she gives us every day.

To begin this ceremony, shamans open sacred space by burning fragrant herbs, shaking a rattle, and speaking words of blessing and invocation. On a square of gift-wrapping paper, they carefully place natural objects like flower petals, seeds, and leaves, creating a beautiful mandala-like design, speaking whatever words of gratitude or reverence come into their hearts while adding each new layer. At the end of the ceremony, they burn the despacho in a fire, requiring everyone to turn their backs to the fire so that the Earth Mother can eat the offering in peace.

One of the very special aspects of being human is our ability to do things simply because they are beautiful and meaningful. Although we may hold a wish in our hearts when we make an offering, there is no guarantee that the offering will secure the object of our desire. Instead, the very act of making the offering reminds us that we already have everything we need, and puts us in touch with a sense of gratitude for all that is. Making offerings also teaches us to be generous, and stops us from clinging too tightly to material objects we consider precious. It wakes us up to the fact that true wealth is measured in how much we give away.

I like to make offerings every day. When I was studying with Wixarika shamans in Mexico, my teachers showed me how to make prayer arrows—beautiful arrows made of sticks and feathers wrapped in colored yarn and adorned with herbs, flowers, crystals, and other natural objects. These arrows are then placed out in nature to bless the land, or to call in blessings from Spirit. Sometimes, offerings are much simpler—a pine cone, a piece of quartz, or several strands of hair left at a significant place and charged with love and intention. My most common offering is tobacco, either placed on the ground or smoked and blown toward what I am blessing. Sometimes—for instance, when I visit a particular sacred Toltec site—I offer something of serious value to me like a treasured crystal, a beloved feather, or even a $100 bill.

When I feel stressed or out of resonance with my highest possibility, making an offering brings me right back to where I want to be. It reminds me of how rich I really am—rich enough to feel grateful, and rich enough to give something back. My shamanic students who struggle with an illusion of scarcity often experience remarkable benefits from establishing a practice of making offerings, realizing the abundance with which they are surrounded at all times. When we make offerings, we affirm that we have enough, we do enough, and we are enough—every moment of every day.

Practice: Giving Back to Spirit

Establish a practice of making an offering every day. Your offering can take the same form every day, or you can experiment with different forms of offerings depending on where you are and what you are doing. Here are some ideas to get you started.

- ◆ In the morning, do as the peoples of the Andes do; offer your first sip of coffee or tea by pouring it on the ground. As you do so, say or think a few words of gratitude for the life force that sustains you, for the day, for your surroundings.

- When you cook outdoors, set aside a small portion of the food to give as an offering to the earth from which the ingredients grew.

- Set aside a portion of your income to give to charity every month. Notice how wealthy you feel when you realize you can afford to give even a small amount away.

- Gather flowers, seed pods, shells, and other natural objects, and arrange them carefully at the base of a tree, on the bank of a river, or in another place that is special to you, knowing that they will eventually decay or be scattered in the wind.

- When visiting ruins or a burial site, make an offering to the ancestors and the guardians of that place.

- Consciously recall all the people who are yet to be born, and make an offering for their happiness and well-being.

Regardless of what type of offering you make, the important thing is to make it with sincerity and an open heart. Don't just set down your offering and rush off to your next task. Take a moment to be fully present, and to speak or think a few words of gratitude and benevolence. Remember, your time and attention are part of the offering too!

Repeat this practice with earth and fire. If you live in a place where fire (in the form of burning wood) is no longer an everyday presence, think about heat and energy instead.

The Extraordinary Practice of Silence

The great yogi Paramahansa Yogananda once wrote: "Through the portals of silence, the healing sun of wisdom and peace will shine upon you." I find his use of the word "portal" very compelling. It characterizes silence as a gate through which we pass to reach a heightened state of awareness. To some of us, this gate is very imposing, and we'll do almost anything to avoid passing through it. We are used to such a high level of stimulation—social media, movies, books, podcasts, or the chattering of our own minds—that we feel frightened and lost when confronted with silence. Yet when we sink into silence, wisdom and peace fall upon us as simply and easily as the rays of the sun.

Watching your mind's attempts to fill silence is both humbling and instructive. You soon realize that your mind believes it needs to stay busy at all times. If it has nothing to do, it will find something to do—usually in the form of worrying, gossiping, identifying problems to be solved or tasks to be carried out, replaying events that have already passed, or rehearsing events that may never happen at all. Like an overeager employee, the mind thinks it has to be productive at all times, even when what it's doing is completely useless.

Just as choosing to abstain from food during a fast can sharpen your senses, settle your spirit, and help you process your emotions, choosing to enter a period of silence creates space for wisdom to flower. This is why shamans, monks, yogis, and other spiritual practitioners make silence an integral part of their spiritual practice. When the conscious mind realizes that it doesn't need to be so busy all the time, it quiets down, allowing deeper insights to bubble up from far below. Indeed, many artists, musicians, and engineers find that they make their greatest breakthroughs and experience their greatest inspiration immediately following a period of silence.

Here are two practices that give you the opportunity to cultivate a taste for silence, and put yourself in the path of the wisdom it brings. Be aware, however, that being silent does not mean just refraining from speaking. It involves allowing your emotions to settle and your mind to grow quiet.

Practice: Sinking into Silence

This practice can help you cultivate a taste for silence and realize its power to bring you wisdom and peace.

1. Choose a period of time in which to be silent. If you are new to the practice of silence, you can start with an hour, then move on to several hours. Or you can just dive in and begin with a full day of silence. Eventually, you will be able to do a silent retreat of several days.

2. During your time of silence, refrain from speaking and vocalizing, as well as from reading, listening to music or podcasts, watching TV, or interacting with screens.

3. Watch what your mind does when you stop flooding it with human-made words and images. Do you feel bored? Restless? Irritable? Calmer and more at peace? Happier?

4. Allow these feeling to change throughout your period of silence. Does being silent get harder or easier as you go along?

5. Turn your attention to your awareness and your sense of aliveness and just be with it without interpreting, analyzing, judging, or commenting on your experience. See if you can cease the narration for even a few minutes. Do

you really need a constant stream of narration for your life to be meaningful?

6. Notice where your attention goes when speech and other stimuli are unavailable. Do you become more attuned to plants and animals? To your breath and body? Does your inner chatter get more pronounced and insistent? Or does your mind quiet down?

If possible, arrange to spend a longer period of silence in nature, whether on a camping trip or just a day hike in the woods. Allow the wisdom of silence to saturate your consciousness.

Practice: Living with Silence

Once you have realized the power of silence, you have to learn how to integrate it into your life in a hectic and noisy world. This practice can help you do that.

1. Begin with just a minute of silence every hour or a few times a day. You can set a timer on your phone or watch to go off hourly, or at least four or five times a day.

2. When the timer dings, immediately stop what you are doing. Stop the dialogue in your

head, the narrative, and focus on your awareness of being alive. Don't think. Just be.

3. Hold this for as long as you can without
thoughts intruding. Most people are hard-
pressed to make it twenty seconds. Do your
best. Dismiss any thoughts that arise and try
again.

4. That's good for now. Try again in an hour.
Obviously, if you are on the phone with a client or in a meeting, you may have to postpone
your date with silence until you are free. Just
don't forget to do the practice.

5. Poco a poco, little by little, learn to extend
your silence for a bit longer.

Conclusion

As we come to the bottom of this treasure chest of extraordinary practices, I hope you feel inspired, empowered, and *excited* to put these tools to work in your own life. Although you may initially find yourself drawn to one set of practices more than others, I hope you return to this book again and again, discovering the benefits of the preparatory, energetic, physical, relational, creative, and perceptual categories of spiritual practice. You may even find yourself mixing and matching practices from different sections, creating a spiritual program that is as unique as you are— and as powerful.

The process of writing this book has been a joyful one for me, as I have been able to review practices that have brought me so much value over the years. It has helped me to clarify aspects of them that I had not articulated before. I hope that your own creativity has been sparked and that you will use it to discover other practices that rise up out of your own being, and that you will share these with others.

I am grateful to you for being drawn to this book and bringing your shining presence to it. My deepest desire is that it will help to preserve age-old, although perhaps obscure, practices from truly superb shamanic and mystical teachers and breathe new life into them at a time when the world needs them so much. Thank you for contributing to this worthy endeavor.

By working with these extraordinary practices on a regular basis, you can come to discover the stages of awakening that the masters and spiritual adepts passed through on their journey of self-realization. You may even realize that, on some level, you are them, and they are you. After all, is there really any difference between "your" process of awakening and someone else's—even those from centuries past? I believe that waking up is simply a process of tapping into a reality that is present and available to all people, at all times. My hope is that, if you've read this far, you've realized that the illusion of separation is just that—an illusion. When anyone engages in spiritual practice, anywhere, it benefits all beings. May your practice benefit all beings, just as the practice of others benefits you.

I bow in gratitude to all the shamans, mystics, saints, sages, avatars, healers, and spiritual pioneers who developed these extraordinary practices over millennia. And I bow to you for your willingness to receive them. I hope that you become ever more conscious of the divinity within you and around you. May you use the enhanced energy, clarity, inner peace, and selfless love arising from these practices to relieve suffering and spread joy wherever life carries you. It is my sincerest intent that your spiritual progress cause positive changes that touch the entire universe.

May you use these powerful tools to build something beautiful. May you and your loved ones be blessed with truth, love, and wonderful energy. I acknowledge you and see you in your perfection, in your beauty, in your right to be here, and in your multidimensional self.

Index of Practices

Part Three: Relational Practices

Part Four: Physical Practices

Part Five: Creative Practices

Part Six: Perceptual Practices

Acknowledgments

I wish to acknowledge all the powerful spiritual teachers, shamans, and mystics living and historical, including my personal guides who so generously helped me and shared their knowledge with me. Here is a partial list of all who have contributed to this book in some way. You can also use the list as a bibliography of sorts that can lead you to further reading.

C. G. Jung
Rupert Sheldrake
Rupert Spira
Ramana Maharshi
Paul Selig
The Qero
The Shipibo
Herlinda Agustin Fernandez
Enrique Flores Sinuiri
The Toltecs
Sergio Magaña
The Wixarika
Don Guadalupe Candelario
Rafael Candelario
James Endredy

Tom Kenyon

The Michael Teachings

Pierre Teilhard de Chardin

Sarah Chambers

Lewis Bostwick

Jesus of Nazareth

Sri Aurobindo

Thich Nhat Hanh

Paramahansa Yogananda

Siddhartha Gautama

Tulku Urgyen Rinpoche

Lahiri Mahasaya

Swami Sri Yukteswar Giri

Chief Seattle

Black Elk

Red Hawk

John Milton

Rumi

Satnam Khalsa

Lao Tsu

John of the Cross

Teresa of Avila

James Nestor

Wim Hof

Randolph Stone

William Blake

Richard Bartlett

About the Author

José Luis Stevens completed a ten-year apprenticeship with a high-degree Wixarika *maracame* in the mountains of Mexico, and has specific training with Shipibo shamans in the Amazon and in the Andes regions of Peru. He has studied with and visited shamans in central Australia, Nepal, Finland, and the American Southwest. He holds a doctorate in counseling psychology from the California Institute of Integral Studies, as well as a master's degree in clinical social work from the University of California, Berkeley. He runs a coaching and consulting business based on the principles outlined in his books, and brings over fifty years of experience to his many clients through effective guidance programs, retreats, trainings, and seminars.

José and his wife Lena are the founders of the Power Path School of Shamanism, which provides webinars, articles, forecasts, and a wide variety of shamanic information. They are the authors of *Secrets of Shamanism: Tapping the Spirit Power Within You.* In addition to numerous other books and articles, José is the author of *How to Pray the Shaman's Way*, *Encounters with Power*, *Awaken the Inner Shaman*, *The Power Path*, and *Transforming Your Dragons*.

Stevens's base of operations is in Santa Fe, New Mexico. He lectures internationally on a number of topics, including principles of power, prosperity, personality types, communication styles, peak performance, and self-development. He has consulted with individuals and businesses in Japan, Canada, Venezuela, Iceland, England, and Finland, and both he and Lena have led many tour groups to the ancient sacred sites of Egypt, England, the Yucatan, and Peru.

Stevens consults with lawyers, business leaders, scientists, life coaches, spiritual teachers, and entrepreneurs throughout the world, as well as with producers, actors, and screenwriters. He uses his knowledge of shamanism and business psychology to coach and assist leaders in making difficult life decisions and developing business strategies. Learn more about his work at:

www.thepowerpath.com

Also from Hierophant Publishing

FOREWORD BY DON JOSE RUIZ

JOSÉ LUIS STEVENS, PhD

HOW TO PRAY THE SHAMAN'S WAY

ANCIENT
TECHNIQUES FOR
EXTRAORDINARY
RESULTS

Available wherever books are sold.

Also from Hierophant Publishing

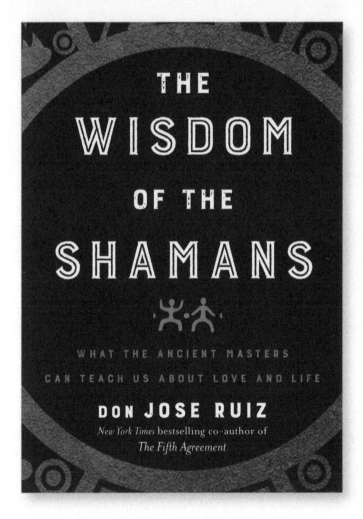

Available wherever books are sold.

Also from Hierophant Publishing

THE MEDICINE BAG

SHAMANIC RITUALS & CEREMONIES FOR PERSONAL TRANSFORMATION

DON JOSE RUIZ

New York Times bestselling co-author of
The Fifth Agreement

Available wherever books are sold.

Hier🜨phant publishing
books that inspire your body, mind, and spirit

San Antonio, TX
www.hierophantpublishing.com